START WITH THE FUTURE AND WORK BACK

A Heritage Management Manifesto

Bruce Weindruch

Hamilton Books
An Imprint of
Rowman & Littlefield

Lanham • Boulder • New York • Toronto • Plymouth, UK

To Dennis Jenks
For believing in the business.

To Susan Grant
For believing in me.

CONTENTS

FOREWORD

During my long career, I have worked at four Fortune 500 corporations with rich histories, but I never fully appreciated how they became great organizations until I met Bruce Weindruch. That was nearly three decades ago, when I was named executive director of public relations at the iconic Sara Lee Corporation.

Sara Lee corporate offices were located in the elegant Three First National Plaza, one of the highest-price-per-square-foot buildings in Chicago's Loop. As the corporate office grew, additional space was desperately needed, so I was asked to work out what to do with two rooms full of file cabinets and memorabilia that had been randomly dumped in coveted office space. Fortunately, I remembered hearing about Bruce Weindruch's company, and the rest is how history is made and preserved.

A few weeks later, the mostly ignored Sara Lee "archives" were loaded onto a large truck headed to Washington, D.C.

Archivists at The History Factory enthusiastically spent the next several months organizing and interpreting the amazing background of the consumer products conglomerate that had grown out of the acquisition of such iconic brands as Hanes, Isotoner, Kiwi, Fuller Brush, Ball Park, Jimmy Dean, Hillshire Farm and Coach Leatherware.

Eventually, instead of sending an assistant to spend hours or days lost in file cabinets, we simply called The History Factory and got exactly what we wanted—and more. In addition to the information needed, we often received additional historical context ranging from correspondence between the company's founder and those who founded similar legendary brands that had been acquired.

During one of his visits to Washington, D.C., Sara Lee Corporation CEO and Chairman John H. Bryan indicated he had an hour of free time, so he asked us to arrange a visit to the archives. The archivists thought he would never leave: He continued to find more and more interesting documents and artifacts.

When I moved to another then-great American corporation, Sears, Roebuck & Company, I encountered a similar archive opportunity. Unlike Sara Lee, Sears had a couple of archivists who had been preserving its historical materials—but the old-fashioned way. The History Factory eventually received two truckloads of documents and artifacts to organize and preserve. Sears began using its history to remind customers that its retail heritage touched every aspect of American life. My favorite initiative created by Bruce and his team involved creating a web-based archive of information about the nearly 75,000 Sears mail-order kit houses that could be delivered to your lot for assembly during the first half of the 20th century. This archive, complete with designs, floor plans and construction details, has been invaluable to owners of Sears homes, who have started clubs around the country devoted to these extraordinary houses.

Needless to say, I am a believer in the premise that truly knowing about the past history of your company can help build a stronger organization in the future. In this book, you'll learn about the power of great storytelling, the surprisingly forward-looking nature of archives, and the many formats and channels through which your organization's history can be creatively and effectively communicated. And along the way, you'll have some fun learning a little bit about the slightly unconventional history of Bruce Weindruch and his colleagues at The History Factory.

Bruce is one of the great storytellers in the world today. He probably knows more about his clients' companies than anyone, except perhaps the founders of those firms. He is a true modern-day chronicler who helps companies envision their futures by understanding and honoring their past. Sit back and enjoy this story about a unique company and its equally unique founder.

Ron Culp

Consultant and Professional Director
Graduate Program in Advertising
and Public Relations
DePaul University

INTRODUCTION

Corporate History in a Blurred World

An influential client of mine, Barry Deutsch, once gave me an invaluable piece of advice. "Don't ever sell a product," he told me. "Sell what you believe. Sell a philosophy."

This was back in the early 1990s, when my company, The History Factory, was a great idea in the midst of becoming a great business. I'd founded the company in 1979 with a very simple goal in mind. I wanted to help organizations capture and use their corporate memories to address current challenges and achieve future goals.

That's what The History Factory was and continues to be to this day. We help our clients extract the maximum amount of value from their history.

Back then, I had a bad habit of walking into sales meetings with bags full of samples. Books. Pictures. Newspaper clippings. Magazines. Videotapes. Anything and everything I could find to help me show people what history could do.

It got so bad—with me lugging around my overstuffed book bag like I was some kind of traveling salesman—that Barry started calling me "the Willy Loman of History."

One day he asked me a simple question: "If you had to go see a client to sell them on a project and you couldn't bring anything with you, what would you do?"

I said, "I guess I'd just talk to them."

"About what?" he asked. "What would you tell them?"

"I'd tell them about what we do and how it can help them," I said. "I'd tell them stories about their history, why it's valuable and how they can use it."

To which he replied, "Exactly. Why don't you just do that?"

This book you're holding in your hands is me without the props. No gimmicks. No crutches.

You're getting it straight and unfiltered.

This is what—and how—I think about corporate history.

And thus this book isn't organized like your typical business tome. You can read it from start to finish, and you'll find that it tells a story about the evolution of my thinking on corporate heritage as well as the changes that have taken place at The History Factory over the years.

But you can also pick it up, flip to a subject you're interested in—or one that might be beneficial to the growth of your organization—and discover that each chapter stands on its own, completely self-contained and usable in its own right.

At The History Factory, we stress the importance of usability, so I've written what I hope is a book that can be approached in whatever way you see fit.

The style and structure, however, are uniquely my own creation.

Think of this book as my own personal jam session on the importance and utility of corporate history.

As you will see, I have a great interest in all kinds of music, especially improvisational music. When great musicians get together to jam, they instinctively draw connections between the music they're currently playing and the music that inspired those sounds.

If you have an ear for this sort of thing, you can hear all of the progressions and chords that have influenced those musicians over time. They're constantly veering from the present to the past and back to the present again. In and out. Out and in. In and out. Which is precisely what history does. It doesn't follow predictable patterns. It flows. It riffs.

It runs—to borrow a line from singer-songwriter Peter Gabriel—in tandem with the random.

To the uninitiated, improvisational music can sound like a jarring clash of sounds. And in a similar regard, the sheer amount of content and data currently streaming into—and out of—organizations on a moment-by-moment basis can look and feel, even to the savviest of communicators, like an incomprehensible blur.

When organizations have a sense of their history, that blur begins to look a lot less hazy. Time slows down like something out of *The Matrix,* and they soon gain clarity of precisely where they were and where they want to go.

Our clients begin to see through the blur to the things that have value. And once we've helped identify the stories, characters and events from their past that are potentially beneficial, they can start using them to their advantage.

Their history becomes found capital, something uniquely valuable and uniquely their own.

Over the course of this book, I'll outline the different ways that organizations can extract value from their history. Some can benefit by preserving their history—building better archives, conducting oral history programs and recording history in real time. Others should consider communicating their history in more effective ways, through the creation of physical exhibits, videos, books or digital content.

But this much is undeniable: In today's business environment, an organization's history simply can't be ignored. It will be praised or scrutinized, used or abused, depending on how an organization cultivates it and the ways in which it is disseminated.

Winston Churchill said it best over a half century ago: "History will be kind to me, for I intend to write it myself."

He certainly did. And so should every forward-thinking organization.

And when I say companies should go out and communicate their history, I mean tell a story. Something with interesting characters and drama and triumph and meaning embedded in it. Something that's both authentic and relevant—the sort of thing that gets people engaged and inspired. Something that creates a buzz.

I have no interest in writing history for history's sake. There are plenty of skilled academics capable of doing that sort of thing. But I don't believe dry, non-strategic corporate histories serve the real-world needs of corporate America.

What good is history, after all, if no one reads it?

When I think of the history of any organization, I think of it as a powerful catalyst for making things happen. I am the descendant of generations of skeptical, no-nonsense businesspeople, so I'm genetically predisposed to be on the lookout for tangible outcomes. An effective corporate heritage program absolutely must yield a good return on investment.

Every client has a particular need at a particular time. For some, it's the need to bolster slumping morale or improve shareholder relations. For others, the goal is to ease the tensions of a complex merger or seek inspiration for an advertising campaign.

Good corporate heritage programs can do all of the above, especially if compelling storytelling is at the heart of that process.

But in order to extract maximum value from history, you have to be very purposeful in crafting the stories you're telling.

You have to think like a marksman. Identify a target. Figure out what you want to hit. How you're going to hit it. And then strike the bull's-eye.

At The History Factory, we have a term for that process. It's called Start with the Future and Work Back™.

Let me show you how—and why—it's done.

1

START WITH THE FUTURE AND WORK BACK

The Art and Utility of Historical Storytelling

"Start with the Future and Work Back" is our guiding philosophy as well as a methodology we employ to create every single deliverable we produce, whether it's a website, a book, a video, an exhibit or a single Tweet.

In short, it's our DNA. Who we are and what we do.

Start with the Future and Work Back has nothing to do with predicting what might happen tomorrow. We're not futurists. It's simply a tool for understanding our clients' current needs and then working backward to help meet them.

In other words, it's our way of exploring the question, "What are you doing today to try to get to tomorrow?"

We start by asking our clients the right questions up front: What are you doing today that makes you so competitive? Who are you trying to reach with your products and services? What are your goals, and what do you want to achieve? How do you want to be viewed by your clients and the world around you?

Once we get the answers to those questions, we conduct highly targeted historical research with those answers in mind—focusing with laser-like precision on creating compelling programs and deliverables that support the strategic objectives our clients just outlined.

History is an interpretive process. It isn't carved in stone. The facts and names and dates stay the same, but the stories themselves should be continually reinterpreted and told in ways that keep them relevant.

Think about Shakespeare's play *Henry V*. Its text has not changed significantly since it was written more than 400 years ago. Same characters. Same plot. Same dialogue. But each generation has chosen to interpret that text in its own way, whether it was Laurence Olivier's defense of Britain in 1944 or Kenneth Branagh's more modern adaptation in 1989, which tried to portray King Henry as an everyday Brit thrust into the spotlight.

The history of the Battle of Agincourt or the Hundred Years' War hasn't changed either, but how we interpret them has changed dramatically.

Organizations have every right to curate their own history—to start with their vision for the future and work back—in the same way.

Academic historians do it all the time. They can't document everything about the Hundred Years' War, so they delve into the research with an eye toward specific facets of that story that are both interesting and relevant to contemporary readers.

In a practical sense, I think businesspeople tend to intuitively connect with Start with the Future and Work Back because it gives them an excuse not to look backward. They continue looking forward. And The History Factory takes care of the rest. By the time we've begun our research and pulled a client's history forward, we've all agreed on a set of objectives.

It's an extraordinarily flexible methodology, which helps us meet every client's needs in a targeted way.

Let's say, for instance, a client tells us that it's worried about the specter of increased government regulation. Fine. No problem.

We go back into their history and start pulling things forward.

We look for things our client did in the past that eased the minds of regulators, government officials and the public at large. We might focus on pulling forward stories that capture its record of community service. Or highlight its progressive hiring practices or the quality of its employee benefits. We still tell our client's whole story, but we make sure to prioritize certain aspects over others.

Or say, for instance, a client is experiencing a great deal of consolidation in its industry. Fine. Now we go in and start pulling forward stories about our client that show it was an exemplary corporate parent or a considerate merger partner. We talk about the strong relationships it has forged with clients and its legacy of innovation. We focus on stories illustrating how it has welcomed new acquisitions and how it has been a great company to work with—and for—over the years.

I can give busy executives an extended menu of reasons—from A to Z—as to why it's in their best interest to leverage their past. History, after all, is a permanent record of an organization's decisions. It can protect valuable trademarks and patents. It helps organizations recruit and retain the best talent available. It can inspire a workforce or act as the foundation for new product development.

But whenever I show our clients how their history—the inventory of experiences they already own—can help them meet specific organizational goals, I'm giving them something of greater value. I'm making their history relevant and valuable to them in the here and now.

And the best part, from a purely bottom-line perspective, is that our clients already own their history. They don't have to pay anything for it. It's theirs, a unique record of who they are and what they've done, just waiting to be packaged into stories that will get them closer to who they want to be and where they want to go.

Personalized Insurance: The Story of The Hartford

When you think of insurance, one of the first companies you're likely to think of is The Hartford. It's a 200-year-old icon. Who wouldn't know The Hartford stag when they saw it? So when people look at The Hartford, they tend to say, "Hell, they *are* the insurance industry."

But by the time The History Factory got to The Hartford in 2009, just after the housing collapse and the onset of the Great Recession, the world had changed. Although the company was about to celebrate 200 years in business, a momentous achievement, it also found itself wrestling with a unique set of challenges. Not only was The Hartford under protection from the Troubled Asset Relief Program (TARP) and undergoing a leadership transition, its leaders were also concerned that its agents were feeling increasingly disenfranchised from the company.

When we ran an anniversary planning session with The Hartford's executives, they made it clear one of the company's primary goals was to strengthen its relationships with independent agents, who had long been responsible for maintaining and bringing in new business.

We had our target. It was time for us to journey back into The Hartford's history and discover the story from the perspective of the agents instead of the company itself.

We were well aware of the fact that The Hartford had insured Abraham Lincoln, which seemed like a good place to start. But we had a lingering question, which we posed to The Hartford's communication team.

"Do we know," one of our researchers asked, "the name of the agent who actually wrote the Lincoln policy?"

Everyone in the meeting looked at each other quizzically, scrambling for an answer, until someone finally piped up and admitted they had no idea.

But within a matter of days, The History Factory did.

After digging into The Hartford's archives, we came upon Lincoln's original policy, which was written by an agent named James L. Hill—a man whose story remained virtually untold for more than a century.

It was all right there in the files. After being elected president in 1860, Abraham Lincoln withdrew $400 from his account. He pocketed $100 in cash, obtained some negotiable bank drafts for his trip to Washington, and invited James L. Hill into his home to talk about his options.

Lincoln's hope was to immediately take out a property casualty policy covering his home and stable in Springfield, Illinois. Time was of the essence. Lincoln needed to sign off on a policy before leaving for Washington, D.C., so Hill rushed over, surveyed Lincoln's home, and issued him a $3,200 Hartford policy for just $24 down. And the rest, as they say, is history.

For decades, The Hartford had trumpeted the fact that it had insured Lincoln's home. It was an old story. But by shifting the focus onto Hill, that old story took on new life and importance. The story was no longer about The Hartford itself; it was about a single agent who went beyond the call of duty to help a valued customer in need.

We found other stories of industrious agents and packaged them together, creating an integrated corporate heritage program for the company's 200th anniversary. A corporate history book, written specifically with The Hartford's agents in mind, was distributed at sales meetings.

Then we created a series of documentaries. These stories resonated with everyone: agents, small businesses and the general public. They went viral across multiple social media platforms.

Those stories traveled the world because they offered up characters and storylines that people were not only interested in but could identify with on a personal level. They were stories about hard work, trust and the power of relationships. They were about people, not a faceless institution.

Our programs were the building blocks in The Hartford's resurgence after the 2008 housing collapse. Internally, the campaign achieved higher rates of employee participation than any other initiative in the company's history.

But the real moral of The Hartford story, in my opinion, is that history is—and always will be—open to new interpretations.

Relevance is the key. Every organization has a story to tell.

The challenge is finding a way to draw something from your past and using it to achieve a concrete objective in the present.

Or as we like to say at The History Factory, the challenge is always to find a way to Start with the Future and Work Back.

In Search of Authenticity

The origins of Start with the Future and Work Back go back to the founding of The History Factory in 1979. I founded the company with a young graphic designer named Tom West, a Princeton grad with whom I'd worked on a project for the Alexandria Archaeological Research Museum.

To call us naïve would be an understatement of epic proportions. Only a graphic designer and a historian would start a business in what was then the worst economic downturn since the Great Depression.

The philosophy behind our company, which was then called the Informative Design Group, was simple: Use history as a communications tool to inform people.

At that point, we didn't fully understand the power of corporate history. We were, in many ways, idealists. We knew history was something real. That it was authentic—and that authentic content was a rare commodity.

I've always felt that if the information you're trying to communicate is yours, then you stand a better chance of connecting with people. Who, after all, doesn't want to be a part of history in one way or another?

Sometimes ignorance is bliss. We didn't pay much attention to the state of the economy at the time, but inflation was at 11.3 percent, unemployment was higher than it had been at any period in the postwar era, and the savings and loan industry was virtually broke. And here we were wandering around talking about history.

We'd meet with executives and say, "Hi, we're here to talk about how you can use your history." People would look at us like we were crazy. "History? We're about to *be* history. Not interested," they'd say. "But, by the way, we just dismembered our corporate communications department, and there's a big room filled with old stuff. Could you take care of it for us?"

Of course, we said yes. We knew the importance and value of what we were preserving. And besides, no one—and I do mean no one—wanted to talk about history in 1979. Organizations didn't want to do anything that attracted unwanted visibility. They were afraid of looking fiscally irresponsible and self-indulgent. Fortunately, some forward-thinking companies did the next best thing. They asked us to preserve their history instead of risking the chance of losing it.

We had a simple system. We'd take boxes of archival material, load them onto a truck and haul them back to our office, where we went to work cataloging them on a first-generation PC with rudimentary electronic spreadsheets. Clients were delighted to have us free up space and cut down on occupancy expenses. It was a win-win for everyone.

In the beginning, our clients pretty much left us alone. Tom and I used to call each other just to make sure the phones still worked. Then, one of our clients phoned one day and asked if we could go through his company's archive and see if they had any examples of "excellent behavior."

Within 10 days, a second client called and asked the exact same question.

When I asked him what this was all about, he told me that his CEO had just read a book called *In Search of Excellence*—the now-legendary work by Tom Peters and Robert H. Waterman Jr.—and was interested in finding stories about "excellent people doing excellent things."

One of our clients at the time was Standard Oil of Ohio, which happened to be the smallest of the Standard Oil companies but also J.D. Rockefeller's original company. That was a huge advantage. We had a pure, intact collection at our disposal—both rich in detail and expansive in scope.

When we pored over the company's speeches, publications and press releases, we discovered an interesting trend. Whenever the price of crude oil was high, Rockefeller was almost always portrayed as an explorer: a rugged adventurer willing to go to any lengths to find the next hidden reservoir of black gold. Whenever the price of crude oil was low, he became "Rockefeller the Great Marketer," the man who rationalized the market.

That was my a-ha moment. I said to myself, "I see exactly what's going on here. We need to look at our clients' history from the vantage point of where they are right now. They're thinking about what they need to do today to get to tomorrow—and we can use history to help support those goals."

We were working on a brochure at the time, wrestling over how to define our point of view on history. I had been tinkering with ideas regarding the past-future continuum when the phrase just came to me: Start with the Future and Work Back.

I repeated it to myself. "When it comes to history, corporations need to Start with the Future and Work Back." And our guiding philosophy was born.

Mellon Bank: The Artistry of Bank Architecture

The durability of Start with the Future and Work Back was tested almost immediately when we received a call from Barry Deutsch, then the senior vice president of marketing for Mellon Bank.

Barry was one of the first professional bank marketers on the East Coast. Banks had no need for marketing departments before the late 1970s because all their products were intensely regulated. They just existed. Take 'em or leave 'em. But when deregulation hit, banks found they needed innovative men and women to create marketing strategies for those products. Barry proved to be the perfect person for the job.

Barry is a fascinating guy. He's one of the most thoughtful and strategic marketers I've ever met. He was an outsider, a marketing guy, who found a niche in the rapidly changing banking industry of the 1980s.

You always got the sense with Barry that he had his face pressed against the glass—that he knew more about banking culture than second- or third-generation bankers. He understood the power of accoutrements, including precisely what shoes and tie a banker should wear, as well as the importance of industry lore.

Of course, some of the old-guard bankers at Mellon thought he was from a different planet. After all, Mellon was a bastion of conservative banking tradition.

Very few banks had more brass and class back then than Mellon, but in the early 1980s, Mellon was also in an acquisitions mode. It was gobbling up banks left and right, and thanks to deregulation, it could go wherever it wanted.

Every time Mellon acquired a bank, we collected another archive. It was good for us—we grew along with Mellon, as we have with all of our clients. But with these acquisitions came new problems. Some of Mellon's new banks were beginning to make it known that they felt alienated from their new parent company.

When Barry invited us to brainstorm on the topic, we put our newly articulated Start with the Future and Work Back methodology into practice. We encouraged Mellon and its acquisitions to communicate their history as if they were all one unified bank instead of a loose consortium of subsidiaries.

After delving into the archives, we were struck by how many of Mellon's banks used their architecture to project a similar set of values. Mellon's acquisitions might have been located in different parts of Pennsylvania, but they were all housed in buildings that projected an aura of security, stability and financial strength. By focusing on architecture—and thus the shared values within Mellon—we could unify these banks in an honest and interesting way.

When we presented the idea to Barry of creating a photo-rich book titled *Our Architectural Heritage*, he immediately signed on to the project. Always three steps ahead of his competitors, he instinctively grasped its potential.

Every one of Mellon's banks was proud of its buildings and its heritage, so they actually petitioned to be part of the book. They'd say, "What about our building here in Altoona? And what about this one in Scranton?" And soon these far-flung banks began to feel as if they were part of the Mellon family.

Not only was *Our Architectural Heritage* a beautiful book, we designed it to be a practical marketing tool as well. Every time a VIP would walk into any of Mellon's banks, they were handed a copy of the book. They could walk around the bank and enjoy the architecture while reading about Mellon's shared values. In one fell swoop, Mellon's image shifted from that of an acquisitions machine to a steward of great buildings and important values.

Had we followed the traditional path of starting with the past and working forward, we would have never come up with a unified story for Mellon Bank. But by identifying what Mellon needed and then using its history to support those goals, we took an element of its history that it never bothered to think about—its architecture—and imbued it with unforeseen value.

Corporate Anniversaries: Building a Better Birthday Cake

More often than not, corporate anniversaries provide clients with a unique opportunity to take stock of where they've been and where they are going. Anniversaries are natural crossroads, a bridge between the past and the future that allows Start with the Future and Work Back to reveal its full potential.

We've worked on highly integrated corporate anniversaries for clients in just about every industry you can think of, from consumer goods, pharmaceuticals and financial services to retail, technology and business services. Today, corporate anniversaries are viewed almost universally as opportunities to drive growth and achieve key objectives. But things were far different in the early 1980s.

At that time, there was a prevailing attitude among corporations that their anniversaries had to be internal affairs. Most organizations were content simply to throw anniversary-themed parties and manufacture commemorative tchotchkes rather than use their birthdays to meet concrete objectives.

These early programs simply honored the past instead of leveraging it for the benefit of the company. And that bothered me.

As a student of business history, I knew that anniversaries held far more potential. All I had to do was dig through the archives we were curating and I would read, in detail, about how some of America's most prestigious companies had chosen to celebrate their anniversaries in the past.

In the 1920s and '30s, for instance, insurance companies often created special policies embossed with eye-catching anniversary logos. Salesmen would fan out in droves—special policies in tow—and use the anniversary-year fanfare to drum up bigger sales and push through new initiatives.

A year later, you'd inevitably see a picture of the company president standing next to a desk stacked to the rafters with new policy orders. The captions would read, "Thank you to our sales force for meeting our anniversary challenge and selling X number of policies. It will indeed be a year to remember."

Throughout much of the 20th century, corporate anniversaries were about driving results, not giving away free stuff. So we began pushing our clients, ever so gently, to remember the importance of Start with the Future and Work Back.

We began asking simple questions like "Have you thought about having a sales contest?" and "You can have an anniversary bash, but why don't you make sure your salespeople have to hit a particular sales target in order to get invited?"

Or we would say, "Do you have any new products that are going to be coming out during your anniversary year? Why don't you brand the hell out of that—and make it a special anniversary-year launch?"

The strength of our argument began to change when we developed our own set of performance-based metrics. This was in the early 1980s, well before the Internet had taken off, so all we offered were rudimentary metrics, but they were important nonetheless.

In those days, we would measure things like how often an anniversary provided face time for a CEO and his people. We'd look at how many anniversary books were accepted by school libraries, as well as how many people actually showed up to watch a particular corporate anniversary video.

In essence, we created metrics to prove that our integrated programs could provide greater return on investment than a few internal parties and a free paperweight or two.

In time, we proved our case.

Take Texaco, for instance. In the early 1990s, we received a call from someone in the company's communications department about helping plan an upcoming anniversary celebration for the company's UK subsidiary.

We were intrigued. Texaco's history is rich and engaging. But when we showed up in London, we discovered a big problem. During our first meeting, the communications department confessed that it knew absolutely nothing about the British side of their history.

The history of oil in Texas? They had that down cold. They could spin some wonderful yarns about their work in Texas, but in regard to the company's history in Britain, the well was dry.

I conceded that celebrating a 50th anniversary in Britain without knowing its history did, indeed, pose a problem, but I promised the team that if there was a history to be found, we'd unearth it.

And we did.

We discovered that Texaco had originated in Britain with the acquisition of a company called Regent Oil. As it turned out, Regent Oil had a colorful history that fed right into Texaco's current-day expansion needs.

Regent had been the brainchild of an amazing entrepreneur named Simon Vos. Not unlike Marcus Samuel, the founder of Shell Oil, Vos was a Jewish businessman looking to find a niche in a highly stratified British society that offered few opportunities for outsiders.

Vos was a great character. He was a jobber. He had spunk and intelligence. Vos bought spot oil on the market and put it out there for sale to a whole bunch of rough-and-tumble types who needed it. And he made a fortune, creating a company that grew so valuable that it captured Texaco's attention in 1956.

When we unearthed everything we could find about Vos and we presented the findings to our client, he was absolutely blown away. I remember him saying, "Wow. You mean, we have a real founder? And an origin story?"

"Yes, you do," I said. We could have just given them facts and dates, but we gave them a founder instead. We gave them an individual—a real character—who became the centerpiece of a successful anniversary campaign that proved to have global reach. In essence, Start with the Future and Work Back gave Texaco a piece of its own history back.

The Great Misunderstanding: Reputation versus Image

Over the years, in trial after trial, Start with the Future and Work Back has never failed us, in large part because it gives our clients a chance to see their history from an entirely new perspective.

That's a powerful thing, in part because so many organizations get confused over the difference between their image and their reputation.

People tend to think they're the same thing, but in reality they're not.

Image is created in the present. Reputation is built over time.

And don't trust anyone who tells you differently.

Years ago, I was invited to attend a corporate identity rollout presented by an influential advertising executive. Her presentation opened with the usual remarks about the strength of her client and how her agency was committed to rolling out a shiny new corporate identity that everyone in the company would be proud to be associated with.

If you've been around as long as I have, you've heard this kind of thing countless times before. But then came a bombshell—what, to my mind, was an impossible, not to mention preposterous, promise.

"Our client," the speaker said, "has told us the reputation it wants, and we intend to build it for them."

Thankfully, I wasn't in the front row, because I almost fell out of my chair. I remember turning to the fellow next to me and whispering, "Did she say reputation? Did she say she's going to build a reputation for them?"

He looked back at me and said, "Yeah, I think she did."

And then, to my astonishment, she repeated herself. "We're going to build you the reputation that you deserve."

Talk about false advertising. I turned back to my neighbor and said, "She'll never do it. She can't build her client a reputation. You build your own reputation. She's totally confusing image with reputation."

And on that point, I was quickly proven correct. Within two months of that presentation, the client was gone, fueled in large part by a mix of legal and reputational issues. Among the company's many sins of hubris was the belief that an advertising agency could conjure a sterling new reputation out of thin air.

The truth is this: An organization's reputation is built, year in and year out, by its actions. It's based on the services the company provides or the products it has created, the quality of its people, and the decisions it has made in the face of major crises.

Don't bother trying to cover up a bad reputation with a glossy new image or branding strategy. It won't work. As advertising legend Bill Bernbach once put it: "Nothing kills a bad product faster than good advertising." The same goes for reputation.

You have to go deeper. You have to show a track record of thought leadership, authenticity and innovation. And that track record is found in one place and one place only: your history.

At The History Factory, we've never told our clients we

could create a new reputation, but we certainly have found a way to shine a spotlight on a reputation they forgot they'd built.

Repent and Reform: The Brooks Brothers Renaissance

The unfortunate truth is that organizations lose sight of their reputation all the time. Consider Brooks Brothers, for example. For a gloomy period from the 1970s into the late 1990s, the most iconic fashion retailer in American history projected a false image of itself, specifically the idea that it was somehow a conservator of classic American values.

That was a huge mistake. We're talking about a clothier here, not Colonial Williamsburg.

In some ways, it was an understandable error. Established in 1818, Brooks Brothers celebrated major anniversaries when the country was embroiled in—or recovering from—major wars: the end of the Civil War in 1868, World War I in 1914, World War II in 1943, and the Vietnam conflict in 1968.

Brooks Brothers may have had a reason to project a patriotic image at various times in its history, but in doing so the company forgot what made it so unique in the first place. Eventually, it bought into a false perception, instead of remembering the reality.

The company may have survived the 1970s and '80s, but by the 1990s most people perceived Brooks Brothers as the official clothier of the establishment. Establishment thinking. Establishment order. Establishment fashions. And if you know anything about the '90s, it's that looking prim and proper and as implacably square as your grandfather was about as compelling to most people as sporting muttonchops and a black top hat.

When we were called in to help the company work on its stodgy image in 2002, we went back into its archive to try to figure out exactly what Brooks Brothers was all about. And as it turned out, Brooks Brothers had built a powerful reputation and loyal following over the years not because it was a conservator of styles but rather because it was a fashion innovator.

Not only did the company introduce ready-to-wear clothes to the American public in 1849, it also tailored the first button-down polo shirt, which was created after one of the Brooks family members noticed British polo players buttoning down their collars to keep them from flapping during matches.

Brooks Brothers salesmen used to dutifully write down in their ledgers what they sold every single day. By poring over those ledgers, we found some amazing stories. Fred Astaire, for instance, used to buy Brooks Brothers foulard ties and use them as belts. When Katharine Hepburn shocked the world and wore pants, she bought them at Brooks Brothers. And when President Franklin Delano Roosevelt wore a striking navy blue cape to Yalta in 1945 for his meeting with Winston Churchill and Joseph Stalin, guess who tailored that cape for him? Brooks Brothers did.

The list went on and on. Jack Dempsey, Cole Porter, Jack Kerouac and Andy Warhol were all Brooks Brothers men. These weren't fashion lemmings. These were trendsetters who turned to Brooks Brothers to create suits, shirts and accessories that commanded people's attention.

When we presented this to Claudio del Vecchio, who had purchased Brooks Brothers in 2001, he said, in a way only Claudio could, "I see who we are now. We will repent and reform."

And they did. We wrote a book called *Generations of Style* with Fred Astaire front and center on page one. And it took on a life of its own. Soon, stories from that book began working their way into stores.

Salespeople internalized these stories, including how a long-tenured associate named Joe Mancini used to have a ticket pocket added to his suit jackets, echoing a tradition from the English gentry. Soon, salesmen began asking for ticket pockets to be sewn into their suits.

Brooks Brothers management recognized the power of these stories. And soon we were asked to spearhead the creation of the Brooks Brothers Institute, which taught employees how to share these stories with customers.

Go into a Brooks Brothers store today and you'll see 26-year-old hipsters shopping for blue chambray slim-cut sports coats alongside nattily dressed baby boomers buying herringbone-gray three-piece suits constructed of luxurious Italian fabrics.

The truth of the matter is that Brooks Brothers, for decades, had taken a far too narrow view of its history. It had allowed a single facet of its history to overshadow a more vibrant tale—a story of daring innovation and nonconformity that resonated with the company's current needs and objectives.

Our work not only helped transform how Brooks Brothers perceived itself but also lifted the spirits of its sales force. Brooks Brothers' values motivated its people to treat customers differently. As fashion innovators, Brooks Brothers salespeople are once again pushing the retailer forward instead of standing back and protecting it, an approach that worked as well almost 200 years ago as it does to this very day.

The Power of the Storyteller:
A Parable for Corporate Heritage

Whenever I think about stories like Brooks Brothers and our Start with the Future and Work Back philosophies, I'm reminded of a wonderful story I was told while working on a project in the Middle East—a part of the world where storytellers are viewed as some of the most important members of society.

It sums up perfectly why we do what we do—and why The History Factory crafts stories out of history the way it does.

According to the story, a young sheik was called upon to take command of a Bedouin army during a great military campaign. Every day, the sheik would lead his men into battle and fight side by side with them, only to return to his camp and find that one man had stayed behind.

This happened for days, until the sheik finally turned to his advisors and demanded to know why the man wasn't joining them in battle. His advisors told him simply that the man was the storyteller.

This didn't impress the sheik. He said, "Get rid of him. He's eating our food; he's wasting a horse. Get rid of him." But his advisors told him, "No. You can never get rid of the storyteller."

Enraged, the sheik demanded to know why. To which his advisors said, "When our men return every day from the fight, the storyteller tells us the story of the battle we have waged. And it's because of the inspiration of his words that we get up the next morning and have the courage to go fight the next battle."

For me, that story of the storyteller is Start with the Future and Work Back in action, a parable about the power of leveraging the past in order to fight the battles that still lay ahead.

AN EXERCISE IN CHARACTER-BUILDING:
THE STORY OF EFFINGHAM B. MORRIS

After the success of *Our Architectural Heritage* for Mellon Bank, the company's corporate communications guru, Barry Deutsch, would huddle with us at the end of every year and put our Start with the Future and Work Back methodology to the test.

We would ask him, "So what are your objectives for next year?" And he would tell us, "We need to do X, Y and Z." And we'd say, "Okay, here's what we recommend."

Barry wanted integration of his programs. Our goal was always to find the right deliverable—whether an exhibit, a book or a presentation—that would best ensure Mellon Bank would hit its target. And he got it.

One of our most challenging Mellon projects, however, came in 1983, when the bank announced that it was acquiring Girard Bank. The acquisition made headlines throughout the East Coast and across the United States.

Girard was to Philadelphia what Mellon was to Pittsburgh. They were near equals, both intensely proud of their patrician heritages. In Philadelphia, when children went to bed, they were taught to pray, "Dear God, please bless Girard Bank, the Pennsylvania Railroad and the Republican party." In that order.

At the time, Mellon's leadership was in a bit of a quandary. Girard's anniversary was coming up, and they didn't know quite how to recognize it. They didn't want to ignore it, but they also didn't want to call too much attention to it because they had just completed the difficult task of forging a unified identity for Mellon Bank.

Of course, Start with the Future and Work Back was an invaluable asset for such a project because it allowed us to pinpoint a new need and then support it with history. Mellon didn't just want to find a connection with Girard. It wanted to push the idea of quality and excellence, two of the buzzwords of the hour.

When we returned to the archives again, we discovered Effingham B. Morris. For many decades, Morris had been a leading light for Girard. There were great stories surrounding him. One day, for example, he walked to Girard's Greek-temple-like headquarters in Philadelphia and saw a group of workmen steam-cleaning the exterior. He purposefully strolled over to them and demanded they stop what they were doing immediately. The cleaners, stunned, asked why. And he said, "It's dark and grimy and old, and it's supposed to look that way. It is not to look new."

We knew we had hit upon something when we dug deeper and found that one of Morris' best-known sayings would work perfectly as an overarching theme for the upcoming anniversary celebration.

Morris used to say, "In all things we do, it's excellence in every detail." It was perfect. It was the theme of "Mellon and Quality" as defined by Effingham B. Morris, a Girard man.

We made Morris a central character in a traveling exhibit built around the idea of Mellon and Quality. This allowed both banks to see themselves as equals. When former Girard executives saw Mellon using quotes from a Girard icon for its new campaign, they were disarmed.

"Look at that," they said. "Mellon is celebrating us, not trying to destroy us."

Some of Mellon's acquisitions had equally interesting characters who were included in the traveling exhibit as well, which further bonded the rapidly growing institution together. It was an off-the-page experience, the kind of traveling exhibit that goes from prestigious museum to prestigious museum across the United States today—only this one stopped in banks.

Even people who weren't Mellon clients stopped in to see the exhibit. It not only brought people through Mellon's doors, it also made current customers feel good about expanding their investments with the bank.

In my mind, the project symbolizes both the flexibility of Start with the Future and Work Back and the enduring appeal of an authentic quote from a strong character—a combination that is as powerful today as it was in 1983.

2

A STOREHOUSE FOR STORYTELLING

How to Build—and Maintain—a Better Corporate Archive

Generally speaking, building an archive isn't a problem. Anyone can save documents. It's maintaining and properly curating an archive that's a far more difficult proposition.

When it comes to archives, I have a theory: The documents that stay around the longest are usually the most inconsequential. And the documents that are most important disappear almost immediately.

Go visit a traditional corporate archive and you'll see exactly what I mean. It's like stumbling upon the British colonial archives. Paper. Paper. Paper. Everywhere. The archive rooms look like they're about to sink under their own weight.

Over the years, old boxes filled with paper take on a certain patina. They begin to look old, and because they look old, it's assumed that they're valuable, making it difficult to determine what's valuable and what's worthless.

That's usually the moment when an archive starts to look intimidating, and someone decides it's time to call in a specialist to separate the wheat from the chaff.

In 2001, Polaroid found itself in just such a predicament.

Originally founded in 1937 by Edwin Land, the company revolutionized the photography market by creating an instant camera that could take and develop pictures—without the need for processing—in less than a minute. Throughout the mid-20th century, Polaroid was an iconic product and brand, so popular in fact that leading photographers from David Hockney to Ansel Adams used to visit Land's New York studio and experiment with his device in hopes of inspiring their next project.

Polaroid's popularity and market share grew throughout the century until the advent of digital cameras brought the company to its knees. By 2001, Polaroid was forced to file for bankruptcy, leaving behind a long line of creditors as well as an archive filled with potentially valuable works of art that no one seemed capable of accurately appraising.

Personally, I was probably more intrigued by the archive's collection of prototype cameras and Land's correspondence than by the artwork, but our job wasn't to seek out items of scientific and historic significance. We were charged with the task of evaluating the net worth of those artistic Polaroids.

In order to get an accurate estimate, we created a unique cataloging process. We isolated 9,000 potentially valuable Polaroids, scanned each of them, identified them, and graded each with a numerical score—1, 2, 3 or 4—based on the reputation of each artist.

We then took our archival breakdown to an independent appraisal firm, which created an item-by-item valuation of the photographs. Based on its estimate, 1,200 photographs were deemed worthy of going to auction at Sotheby's, a sale that was accepted by a U.S. bankruptcy court in June 2010.

Without our efforts, it was likely that a single buyer would have glanced over the scattershot archives and provided a woefully low bid for what was a treasure trove of valuable art. After all, how was Polaroid to know what those images were worth when they didn't even know exactly what they had? By hiring us, they received an accurate appraisal, with the sale of those 1,200 photos netting a cool $12.47 million.

The Record Store of History: Building Archives for Corporate America

At The History Factory, we believe that an archive is the starting place for finding meaning. But more importantly, it's where you go to authenticate who you are as an organization. It provides undisputable evidence that the image you want to project, the values you espouse, and the reputation you've built over time are not only legitimate but completely warranted.

You want to prove that you're an innovative company? Or that you're a trusted service provider? Or that you've been more ecologically minded than any of your peers?

Well, then you're going to have to offer up proof to support those claims. And in order to find—or continue to preserve—that proof, you're going to have to build and maintain a proper archive.

Once armed with carefully curated content, organizations can also generate highly strategic content that addresses a myriad of practical business challenges.

Pick your business objective of choice—enhance a brand, boost morale, reduce costs, accelerate innovation, or recruit new talent—and you'll find that archives are often the linchpin that makes things happen within an organization.

The problem is that most corporations tend to see their archive as a communal dumping ground for every memo, photograph and corporate knickknack that's ever seen the light of day.

That's bad archival management. When properly designed and implemented, a corporate archive distills a vast inventory of historical data into a carefully curated catalog of content that can help any organization see where it's been and where it's headed.

First and foremost, all corporate archives should be graded on their overall usability. Can an organization's decision-makers and communicators quickly and easily gain access to archival content when they need it—in the most efficient and intuitive way possible?

From day one, The History Factory has been continuously testing and building searchable archival solutions so that there are no barriers between our clients and their content.

I'm talking about pure on-demand access to your content. That's what we're after. My goal has always been to eliminate the gatekeepers and directly connect organizations to their content.

This has been a long-standing obsession of mine, with roots that reach all the way back to a three-year stretch in the early 1970s, when I took some time off between high school and college to operate a record store in my hometown.

I was fairly successful at running my store in the primordial pre-iTunes days, because I've always studied the roots of popular music and had an innate feel for musical trends.

Anyone who's read *High Fidelity* by Nick Hornby will recognize the record-store geeks like me who constantly devise top-10 lists and then push themselves to come up with newer, more challenging topics. Top 10 guitar solos? That's easy. What about the top 10 lead guitar solos by a Brit? Or better yet, the 10 best lead guitar solos by a Brit inspired by an earlier lead guitar solo?

This incessant list-making is a form of curation. It's a way of mentally cataloging information so you can more easily make connections between and among songs, artists, genres and styles.

In my store, I curated an inventory made up of thousands of unique bits of content—i.e., record albums—knowing what my customers wanted. More importantly, I built a collection for customers who didn't even know what they wanted until I made the connections for them.

That's the way I process the world. I think like Pandora. You like Nils Lofgren? OK, then you're gonna really like David Lindley. You want to understand the Allman Brothers? Then you must learn the influence of King Curtis. You're into Taj Mahal? Then give Danny Barker a listen. That's exactly how I did it back in the day. I know it's inside stuff. But believe me, I sold a lot of albums that way.

So a good user-friendly corporate archive should be run like a record store. It's all about arranging the content in ways that allow users to spot trends and make connections.

Archival research demands a similar approach, an openness to taking an object, a photo or a receipt and looking for the unforeseen connection—the two dots that everyone noticed but never thought to connect.

Take Cheerios, for example. The General Mills archive had a wonderfully preserved example of the first box, which was introduced on May 1, 1941, as "Cheerioats." While I was impressed that General Mills had shown the foresight to save this heirloom, the box was being housed as a historical relic instead of being used to fulfill a greater purpose.

There, in plain sight, on the side of the box, was the Recommended Dietary Allowance, a landmark requirement that had been instituted by the newly established US Food and Nutrition Board the very month that Cheerioats had been launched.

Looking at that box 50 years later, it became clear to us that General Mills had a great story to tell to mothers across the world—namely, that Cheerios had been born with nutrition as its focus and had retained that focus right up to the present day.

We discovered similarly valuable finds when digging through old bank archives. In one case, we found a badly burned $5 note with a letter dating back to the 1840s, when banks used to print and redeem their own currency.

At first glance, it looked like a charred receipt. But when we gave the note and the letter the attention they deserved, we found that they told a fascinating story. The letter described how a woman of limited means had been caught in a fire. How she had dropped the note and it singed almost to ashes. And how the bank made good on her request to redeem it.

It was a simple archival document. I doubt the bank even knew it existed, but think about what that single find revealed about the character of that bank. Its humanity. Its priorities. The strength of its promises. And its commitment to elevating the needs of its customers above its own bottom line.

The point, of course, is that archives are invaluable repositories of found capital. They're often brimming with historical content that's of great value in the present day. But they also don't confess their wisdom and secrets unless you know exactly how to tease it out of them.

Finding What Can't Be Found:
The Tale of the 30-Year-Old Mustard Bottle

Most organizations tend to overlook their archives until something triggers them to take a second look. There's a great story, perhaps apocryphal, about David Rockefeller that sums up this phenomenon quite nicely.

According to Chase Manhattan Bank lore, after President Richard Nixon opened up limited trade relations with China in 1972, David Rockefeller arranged a meeting with bankers in China. In preparation for the trip, he called a meeting with his aides and asked them if they could go into the company's archives and find an artifact that symbolized the bank's long-standing relationship with China.

Unease filled the room, but Rockefeller continued on. When the meeting was over and Rockefeller went his own way, his aides gathered together, clearly concerned about what they'd just been asked to do.

"What are we going to do now?" one of Rockefeller's aides said. "We don't even have an archive."

In the early years of The History Factory, we built and managed archives the old-fashioned way, with sweat and staple removers. It was all analog all the way. Open up boxes. Flip through card catalogs. Assess. Centralize. Arrange.

This was back when archives were organized according to provenance. You divided up documents according to who created them and from what department they originated. Anything that came from the desk of the CEO—no matter the subject matter—went into Record Group 1: Office of the President and CEO. Press releases went into Record Group 2: Public Relations Department. And so on.

Even back then, I knew it was an ineffectual system that was built by archivists, for archivists. If you were a C-suite executive or communications officer, you had no clue how to find anything in your own archive. Nothing was intuitive. Within the rigid organizational hierarchy, individual files were described in cryptic numerical codes.

If you were interested in trying to get a feel for what it was like to work on an assembly line during World War II, you had to call up the archivist, who was the only one who knew to look for newsletters in Record Group 3, Boxes 4 through 7.

I knew there had to be a better way. So as an early convert to PCs and spreadsheets, I encouraged our employees to start tinkering around with building computer-based archival databases that were categorized according to subject metatags instead of numerical codes. If you wanted to catalog a newsletter that was published during World War II, wouldn't it be better to file it under the descriptor World War II?

Clients immediately liked our databases because we were using language they could understand and because our databases allowed us to fulfill requests at unprecedented speeds.

One day, for example, a sales executive from one of our founding clients, McCormick Spices, called us in a panic. He'd just received a call from McDonald's, one of McCormick's largest clients, informing him that the company was in the process of completing a museum-like replica of one of its early restaurants.

McDonald's was filling the shelves of this "museum" with accurate reproductions of the containers that McDonald's used in the mid-1950s. The request to McCormick was very clear: Find a 1950s-era McCormick five-gallon institutional mustard jar and ship it to McDonald's headquarters ASAP.

The McCormick sales exec was sweating bullets. You could hear it in his voice, but while he was busy stressing the importance of this request from his largest customer, I was clicking through the database. I quickly located two pristine McCormick Spice mustard labels from 1955.

I told our contact at McCormick not to worry. We had his labels right here, as well as a catalog picture of the jar.

We priority shipped the labels to McCormick, which affixed one of the labels onto a five-gallon glass jar, using the catalog picture to get it just right.

And thus, with a few keystrokes and our innovative databases, we preserved McCormick's relationship with its most important client.

The Birth of Online Archives

Our work with McCormick Spices validated our approach to archiving and led to a growing roster of archival clients during the mid–1980s. But despite our successes, I still had grander plans for our databases.

Our homegrown databases were proving to be efficient for us, but they still didn't connect our clients directly to their own archives. Whenever our clients needed something, they had to call or fax us. Then we had to go into our databases, locate the document, scan it and then fax it back.

In the end, we were still acting as middlemen in the exchange. And that inevitably slowed down the process.

I was interested in pioneering a self-service model, creating shared databases that allowed our clients to pull whatever they needed from their archives, whenever they needed it, without outside assistance.

Of course, traditional archivists weren't thrilled with this idea, which threatened their position as information gatekeepers. But I've always felt that the best way to get people to understand the power of archives is to get them to start using them themselves.

When you motivate CEOs, corporate communicators and PR representatives to use an archive, they see its worth. They become converts. And the next thing you know, they're working diligently to save documents themselves and strengthen the archive they've been working from.

In the end, the people who benefit the most from archives contribute the most to archives.

In 1986, as standalone personal computers were starting to be linked together by networks, we saw an opportunity to create a more user-friendly archival program.

We met an enterprising fellow who had developed a software application for professional home remodelers. It was primitive by today's standards but innovative for its day. When estimators were out in the field, they needed a quick and easy way to describe what they were seeing and what they needed in order to create an accurate materials estimate. If Job A required red brick, glass and sand, the estimator simply opened up the file for Job A, clicked on a pull-down materials menu, and clicked on the tags "red brick," "glass" and "sand," and typed in the required amount for each.

When I saw the program, I asked the developer if he could adapt it into an archival database. And he did. Whenever we cataloged or searched for a file, we simply clicked on a pull-down menu of predetermined tags and clicked the appropriate descriptors for that file.

If we were cataloging a memo about environmental regulations from the 1970s from CEO John Smith, we'd go to the pull-down menu and click "memorandum," "environmental," "1970s," and "John Smith." Because the system was network-based, everyone on the network had access to it.

If a client wanted information about environmental regulations, for example, all we had to do was click on the master tab for "environmental regulations" and all the appropriate files would appear.

The program, which we called our "Heritage System," exponentially simplified our archival management process. It was so impressive, in fact, that when we presented it to the legendary strategic thinker Vic Millar, then the head of the newly established Saatchi Consulting, he commissioned us to tweak the system for his firm's new computer network.

Millar's history speaks for itself. He was a visionary leader in Arthur Andersen's management information consulting division for many years. Along with Harvard Business School's

Michael Porter, Millar pioneered the concept of information for competitive advantage. But by the time we met Millar in 1987, he was intensely interested in the idea of continuous online archiving, especially finding a way to bank all of Saatchi Consulting's data and share it with all the employees as quickly as possible.

He believed that corporate information tended to become available in a stair-step pattern. For a given period of time, organizations spent the necessary resources to properly archive their insights (the riser of the staircase) and then, almost inevitably, a period of nonactivity would follow when their archives were neglected (the tread of the staircase). This pattern, he believed, repeated over and over again. A round of archiving, a round of neglect. Decade after decade.

It was during those flat periods, Millar believed, that an organization ran the risk of a competitor stealing its important ideas or missing a growth opportunity. To avoid such pitfalls, Millar wanted to find a way to continuously archive the ideas Saatchi Consulting was generating in real time.

Millar's vision was music to my ears. We were hired to do systems integration work for Saatchi Consulting's new headquarters. We configured Saatchi's first network; then, we went out and did the RFPs for all their computers, loaded our software, and built a networked archival database that was light-years ahead of its time.

Alas, the only problem was the slow network speed and the meager computing power of PCs, which couldn't match the volume requirements of the Saatchi Consulting employees who were trying to use it. Our revolutionary archival solution worked beautifully on Tuesdays between 4 p.m. and 5 p.m. but was monstrously slow just about anytime else. We had the right system but simply not enough bandwidth to support it.

Bringing the Bar Scanner to Boeing

After our promising but ultimately frustrating initial foray into online archiving, I made sure that The History Factory always invested in the leading-edge—if not the bleeding-edge—technologies of the day.

It was Vic Millar who reinforced the importance of accessibility, usability and speed. Sure, it's great to have wonderful content, but we had to ensure our clients had fast and easy access to that data as well.

Luckily, a few years later we got a call from Boeing in Seattle, which was having a difficult time getting ready for its coming 75th anniversary in 1991. Like so many of our clients, Boeing knew it had valuable treasures in its archives but didn't have a clue where the most-important stuff was hiding.

Boeing's records were scattered everywhere. Some were sealed away in warehouses in Seattle. Some with its law firm, Perkins Coie. Some were in Canada due to Boeing's acquisition of de Havilland in 1986, and others were being kept near Philadelphia, where Sikorsky, another of its acquisitions, operated.

To make things more difficult, Boeing informed us that it would like all of the files to be converted into a database as quickly as possible for its anniversary. We immediately recognized that creating the database would be a challenge because it's not easy to stroll through a warehouse with a computer at your side.

Things were looking a bit grim for a moment, but then I started thinking about barcodes. Why barcodes? Because we'd done some work for food manufacturers like Campbell's and retailers like Sears, where we'd seen the scanner and UPC revolutionize those businesses.

Why, I wondered, couldn't we use scanners and UPCs to help Boeing create its database?

Here's how we did it. We sent team members into the warehouse with hand-held scanners—similar to what was being used to inventory store merchandise. They had laminated sheets with UPCs representing different tags for different item types (photos, documents, physical objects, etc.), subject categories (military, commercial, helicopters) and date ranges (1930s, 1940s, 1950s).

Before they opened up a box, they applied a label with a unique UPC to the front of each box and then scanned the UPC. Next, as they identified the contents of each file, they zapped the corresponding UPC on the laminated sheet to catalog the file's type, content and date range. At the end of each day, they plugged their scanners into a computer and downloaded the data right into our databases.

Within days of being in the field, our teams were able to provide Boeing with very detailed reports that quantified how much information they possessed about specific aircraft and innovations. We told them the percentage of their archives relating to 707s, B-52s and so on. We also unearthed valuable finds that laid the foundation for the company's entire 75th anniversary celebration.

I'll never forget one of our discoveries. It was a very early 16 mm film that captured the manufacturing of an airplane at William Boeing's first Seattle shop in the 1920s. After sitting in storage for decades, it didn't have a scratch on it. It was pristine. And it provided a window into Boeing's precision, care and craftsmanship.

We showed it to Boeing executives, and they all said the same thing: Wow. They took the film, duplicated it, and interspersed it with footage of Boeing's contemporary manufacturing processes. You would see women in the 1920s stitching fabric on a wing of an old airplane and then see a 747 with a robot doing the same thing in the 1980s. Next, you would see aeronautical engineers from days past balancing propellers by hand and putting little "inspected by" tags on them. And then you'd see contemporary mechanized lifts weighing giant propellers as data instantly popped up on a computer screen.

It was a three-minute film, but it delivered a powerful message. "What didn't work, Boeing fixed. What did work, Boeing did even better." The final line of the script was perfect: "At Boeing—We make history every day."

And thus, a film that was buried amid thousands of records became the soul and promise for the future of a 75-year-old manufacturing icon.

Archiving The History Factory Way

While the tools and techniques we use to catalog and process archives have evolved radically over the years, most of our core archival practices have never changed. We've stayed true to the belief that our archivists should be trained to both build archives and process client requests.

In terms of pure efficiency, it's better to have one archivist arrange an archive while another fields research requests as they come in—two separate tasks for two separate people.

But if my time in the record-store business taught me any-thing, it's that you have to listen very carefully to the needs of your customers. Thus, I've always felt that it's valuable for all of our archivists to see, read and hear the requests that are coming in from our clients.

Fortune 500 companies and organizations with global foot-prints see and describe the world much differently than academ-ics. We have our own jargon. We value different things. And we place greater value on different kinds of archival research.

We realize that in the modern marketplace, original insights and depth of content matter, which is why all of our archi-vists are responsible for managing multiple collections and are expected to continue overseeing those archives over time.

Not only does this ensure that they know the material inside and out, it also allows teams of archivists, working with our writ-ers, designers and other creatives, to gather together to meet ultra-tight deadlines and client requests.

If an organization had to staff its own in-house archives with all the capabilities that we have at The History Factory, it would have to hire six people to do it right. We spread that cost across our entire organization among multiple clients, greatly reducing the overall expenditures of our services.

Experience matters. And I can say without hesitation that the continual success and evolution of our archival program has its roots in the early 1990s, when we turned our attention to professionalizing our processes.

In the early years of The History Factory, all my energy was poured into meeting clients, creating exhibits, writing and working hard just to make payroll every month.

Because we had a limited number of archival clients, I tended to hire grad students to oversee our archives. If a valued client came asking about a job for their son or daughter, I'd stick their kid in our archives with a few spreadsheets and call it a day.

In all honesty, our archive was the place everyone worked hard to get out of. Everyone wanted to be a creative—a writer, researcher, designer or exhibit creator—where all the action was.

It was in 1989, after we moved our offices to a 75-year-old light-manufacturing building on 15th Street Northwest, in the heart of Washington, D.C., that we rebranded the company. Informative Design Group became The History Factory.

The name was inspired, in part, by the layout of the new site. Archives were located on the ground floor, then slowly evolved as they moved into the higher floors of the building, transforming into books, videos and exhibits. We saw our new space as a factory that refined and processed history into valuable deliverables.

With purpose-built processing space and plenty of archival storage capacity, we set out to hire the best professional archivists we could find. There was no more nepotism. No more friends of friends working in our archives.

Our newly overhauled archival team put in place sound archival principles—absolute best practices—that are still with us today, all while we looked for ways to update our homebuilt Heritage archival software program.

Our Heritage software may have been ahead of its time, but corporations were catching up to us on the technology front. No one wanted bespoke software. Our clients' IT people would look at Heritage and go, "Where's your documentation for this?" We'd say, "We don't have any." And they'd begin to worry.

So we turned to an established off-the-shelf archival software program called Rediscovery. This was at a time when it became increasingly important for our archival system to be compatible with other programs. Rediscovery proved to be the ideal solution. You could take almost any existing corporate software platform and link it up to Rediscovery without a problem. And it worked. It all fit together.

In time, our archival service programs evolved into one of our largest revenue streams. Thanks to our impressive track record, our client list and our new space, we started adding new clients left and right.

By 1994, the economy was booming. It was all about acquisitions, new audiences and growth. Everyone was interested in looking forward, blazing a new trail and creating something new.

As a general rule, any time the economy is growing, it's a good time to be in the archival business, because forward-moving companies are moving so fast that they begin worrying their information will be lost.

So in 1995, we relocated again, this time to a sprawling suburban location in Chantilly, in northern Virginia, that was built for archives. It had everything: finely tuned temperature and humidity levels, UV filters on window surfaces, storage spaces constructed of noncombustible materials, and intrusion protection and access controls with password-protected, electronically activated doors.

Our new home was huge. When we first moved there, we only took up a fraction of the main warehouse space. But as a growing number of clients joined the fold, we expanded upward and outward, growing in size, scope and influence right along with our A-list clients.

The Archival Database of Tomorrow

The problem with Rediscovery was that it didn't get us any closer to my original goal of directly connecting clients with their archives. While we had replaced numerical archival codes with recognizable subject tags and leveraged corporate networks to provide easier access for our clients, Rediscovery still looked and felt like an archivist's tool.

As websites began to utilize richer imagery and navigation options—differentiating their front-end user experience from their mundane back-end coding—I decided it was time for an update.

Intent on staying ahead of the technological curve, we had to make sure our new archival software did more than look good. It had to offer search capabilities that could accurately catalog and scan a growing array of digital formats (PDFs, JPEGs, AVIs and MP3s) that were coming onto the scene.

Fortunately, The Second City comedy troupe approached us in 2005, looking for help with a massive archiving project, laying the foundation for our next archival software package.

The Second City was an interesting client because its archives were being filled with the same kind of content year after year. Since the troupe's inception in 1959, it had banked scripts, tapes of live performances, performer bios, posters and headshots.

By the time we got there, the troupe had expanded north to Toronto and west to Hollywood and possessed the most impressive alumni list this side of *Saturday Night Live.* But its ability to fill requests for archival pictures, videos and headshots from media outlets and Hollywood producers was downright slow and ineffective.

If a request came in for video of Gilda Radner from 1974 or a headshot of Stephen Colbert from 1991, The Second City was likely to have it, but it struggled to find it fast enough. The troupe also lacked a system for quickly archiving the headshots, scripts and shows of the performers who were currently working for The Second City, any one of whom could turn out to be the next Tina Fey or Bill Murray.

Our solution was to build The Second City an archival database that preserved and shared its content in real time. In some ways, the system closely mirrored the real-time archiving system that we'd built for Vic Millar at Saatchi Consulting two decades earlier. But this time, the technology was sufficiently powerful for the concept to work.

On a day-to-day basis, managers from all three locations could drag their revised scripts, videos, updated headshots and directors' notes into our database, click a button, and centralize the materials in a single shared archival hub. Our archival database not only allowed each satellite location to see and experience what the others were doing, it also allowed The Second City to harness a potential new revenue stream by licensing original proprietary assets.

Our work with The Second City led to the creation of our next-generation archival database, which we called LuminARC™.

With LuminARC, clients can log in via a Web browser and follow a very simple tree of subject tags. If a client clicks on a macro subject heading like "offices," the system branches out into subcategories such as "Pittsburgh," "New York" and "Chicago." Click on one of those city subheads and the tree expands again. Next might come the tag "departments" or "leaders" or "communicators."

The system worked beautifully from day one. It's our primary archival processing tool, a cloud-based system that can be customized to meet the needs of any client. It manages every format and material type available, from fading photographs and YouTube videos to old sound recordings and Twitter feeds. It also allows our clients to determine exactly who has access to their archives at any given moment in time, whether it's the entire company or a single user.

For me, running a good corporate archive will always take me back to my record-store days, in part because my own business experience taught me the value of listening to—and then meeting—the needs of the customer. It's about sharing wisdom instead of sealing it up behind closed doors.

If we have a bias at The History Factory, it's toward usability. How can we make a client's archives more useful and easily accessible? How can we construct a matrix of valuable information that connects the dots between where you were and where you're going?

The moral of the story, for me, is that archives are a means to an end. Never the end. Archival work gives someone like me, who's interested in both history and business, a tremendous passion for ensuring the cycle continues.

That's why I always say that archives are the most forward-looking thing we do at The History Factory. It ensures that the insights and wisdom of an organization will be there for future generations, ready and waiting not only to be remembered but to be leveraged to create an even more dynamic future.

TALES FROM THE ARCHIVES: THE WALTER MONDALE AFFAIR

Over the years, we've amassed more than our fair share of interesting archival stories, but nothing quite compares to the day we could have killed Walter Mondale.

This was back in the mid-1980s, when we were working on an archival project for McCormick Spices. We'd been called in to help put its massive archives in order as the company prepared to shutter its landmark headquarters building in Baltimore's Inner Harbor.

It was a stunning archive. I've never seen or smelled anything quite like it. It was filled with tens of thousands of boxes of spice jars and spice labels. Ginger, black pepper, cloves, turmeric. Labels from 1911, jars from 1932, boxes from the 1960s. It smelled like the Canary Islands in there.

After the passage of the Pure Food and Drug Act of 1906, companies like McCormick were compelled to save every label of every package for regulatory reasons. So the company had gotten into the habit of throwing everything into boxes and shoving them into this giant storeroom in its original factory.

We were having a ball going through and cataloging everything, until we received a visit from McCormick's head of safety, who told us there was one problem.

He told us it was going to be our responsibility to dispense with all of the old, dried-up spices as soon as possible, and as far away from the McCormick site as possible. And in order to do it right, we had to fumigate the stuff before we dumped it in the trash.

That was a rather big wrinkle, but over the course of a few hours we came up with what we thought was a brilliant idea. We'd go back to one of the rooms of our three-room suite in D.C. and tape up all the seams—from the floor to the ceiling—bring in all the boxes, drop some cyanide to fumigate the area and leave.

There was only one slight hitch. The office directly adjacent to ours was the national campaign headquarters for presidential contender Walter Mondale. That gave us great pause. If any of the cyanide leaked over into the adjacent office and Mondale happened to be there, we were going to be responsible for killing the Democratic Party's nominee for president and all of his senior staff.

If we didn't do this right, it would grab headlines around the world and forever sully our good names as well as the names of our descendants.

But what can you do? We had a job to do. So we kept our fingers crossed, chose a weekend for the big event when we assumed most people would be away, and did it.

And lucky for us, it worked. Without any casualties. We fumigated the place, stuffed the old spice products into large plastic bags and wheeled them out to the trash.

And as a result, we ensured Mondale got his fair shake at the Oval Office during the 1984 presidential elections.

3

KNOW THYSELF

Oral Histories and the Enduring Value
of Institutional Memories

History is a preserve-it-or-lose-it commodity. Archives are repositories for the written word. They preserve all the ideas and facts that an organization chooses to document.

But what about all the things that were said but never recorded? How do you unearth the motivations underlying past decisions? Or record for posterity's sake the wisdom and philosophies of the people running an organization in the present day?

Answer: You launch an oral history program.

In my experience, some of the most trivial events in the corporate world tend to get documented the most, and some of the most important decisions tend to get documented the least.

Oral histories act like a safety net for all of that valuable information. They're tools for discovery—long, in-depth conversations designed to capture wisdom that rarely gets put to paper.

Oral histories are great for answering the "why" questions.

Why did a company get acquired? Why did it launch one of its products before it was ready? Why did it choose to go public?

As a result, oral histories can be very emotional exchanges. When I conduct oral histories, I have a tendency to frame questions in the present tense. "It's 1973, you just got a call from the SEC requesting a meeting. What do you do? What are you thinking?"

The goal is to take people back to that specific moment in time so that they talk instinctually, without any filters.

My approach has yielded some memorable stories over the years. During one oral history interview in the mid-1990s, I was asking an executive about a challenging period in his company's history, when I noticed that his hands started to fumble around his desk. He was still relaying his story in wonderful detail, but his hands seemed to take on a mind of their own, feeling around for something.

After he completed his thought, I stopped him and said, "Are you OK?"

He quickly snapped out of his trance and said, "You know what? I haven't smoked since 1977, but I felt just now like I really needed a cigarette. I was reaching around my desk for where I used to keep my pack of cigarettes to have a smoke."

I can guarantee you one thing. Future leaders who read the transcript of his oral history will know exactly why he made the decisions he did. They'll not only understand his motivations; they'll empathize with him on a very personal level.

And thus oral histories can forge connections between leaders from wholly different eras, linking together the past and the future in unique ways. But they can also be extraordinary motivating tools.

In the past, employees used to go looking for direction exclusively from those at the top. Today, you have more and more organizations looking to employees to inspire each other.

It all comes back to the democratization of content. Just look at how oral histories have been co-opted in the public sphere. Individual oral histories are being created and read on Facebook and Twitter every single day.

Think about what determines an organization's reputation in today's social media-obsessed climate. A company's reputation is no longer predicated solely on the actions of those at the top; it's now based on the actions of every individual within the organization. Everyone, from the intern on up, is an ambassador for your brand.

And that's why I encourage our clients to find and document history from the bottom to the top of the ladder. Older, more established companies as well as newer organizations can both benefit from recording the thoughts of their leaders and key members of their work force, because stories captured today can have valuable applications in the years ahead.

The Great Turnaround: A Biotech Parable

The great thing about conducting oral histories with young companies is that key players who helped build the company tend to still be around. With older companies, you have to rely on archival information to better understand their origins.

I'm particularly fond of the oral history work we did for a youthful California-based biotech firm named Chiron in 2005.

Chiron, which was founded in 1981, was a pioneer in the field of pharmaceuticals, especially vaccines and blood-testing units. It had grown, like so many other biopharmaceutical companies, by taking a strategic investment, in this case by Novartis. It was a good partnership, but then Chiron slipped up. In 2004, regulators discovered a potential bacterial contamination in the company's influenza vaccine plant in England and suspended the company's license to create vaccines. Its stock price plummeted, and Chiron was virtually written off as a company destined for a slow, steady demise.

But through what the company's CEO called a "superhuman effort," it rebounded over the course of a year, got its licenses back and saw its stock price begin to rise. Seeing this phoenix rise from the ashes and knowing Chiron's share price was only going to climb higher, Novartis figured it had better grab Chiron as soon as possible.

An offer was made. And with no other workable alternatives in hand, management had to accept. In a short time, Chiron was going to be swallowed up by Novartis and Chiron's CEO, Howard Pien, knew it.

Pien contacted us because he didn't want to see Chiron's history get lost in the transition. "My team," he told us, "worked for a year to turn this company around. I want people to know that story. I want a book for all of the people who built this company, particularly the people who worked so hard to save it. I want them all to be remembered."

But there was a catch. The Novartis acquisition would be completed within months. After which, some of the key characters in Chiron's story might be gone. So Pien gave us a hard and fast deadline. "I need you," he told us, "to complete this book in three months. Can you do that?"

Pien realized that was an extraordinarily tight deadline. In order to properly document what had just happened, we were going to have to do a large number of oral histories with employees across the company.

We were going to have to be thorough—and fast.

So he turned to me and my colleague and told us he'd leave us a moment to discuss.

When Pien left, my colleague—knowing me all too well—looked at me and said, "You're going to do it, aren't you?"

And I said, "Yeah, I want to do it."

And we did.

It was a story about everyone at Chiron. The leadership. The researchers. The scientists. It was a history about a 25-year-old company compiled almost exclusively from long-form oral histories, in which we sat down with people and let them tell their own stories from their own perspectives.

It all was captured in that book: Chiron's legacy in pioneering unique products. Its commitment to helping save lives. What it felt like to lose that key revenue channel in Britain. And the company's miraculous turnaround.

In some ways, our work with Chiron is like a message in a bottle that's been set adrift in the ocean. Chiron is now a part of Novartis. It's been absorbed and assimilated. And yet there's always going to be a book that tells Chiron's story. Years from now, some division of Novartis is going to want to trace the lineage of its latest vaccine or blockbuster new drug, and it's going to find that its roots are as much part of Chiron as they are of Novartis. The importance of Chiron and its people will re-emerge.

Similarly, someday Novartis is going to run into a challenge. Some people within the company are likely to say, "We can't overcome this." And then someone is going to pull out our Chiron book and say, "What do you mean, we can't do this? Look at what those guys at Chiron did. If they could do it against all odds, we can do it, too."

That's the power of a good oral history project. It not only preserves the past, it inspires a pathway toward the future.

Conversation as Catharsis: Oral Histories that Can Heal

We've been executing oral history programs at The History Factory for more than three decades, but my own experience conducting oral histories dates back even further—back to when I analyzed the rise and fall of independent auto dealerships for my senior thesis at Grinnell College.

I've always been a motor head. My father appreciated cars, too. When I was young, my dad and I used to spend many of our Saturdays at the local Chrysler-Plymouth dealership, chewing the fat with the guys in the service department in the morning before switching over to the salesmen in the afternoon. My fascination with cars has never faded; I still crave the smell of motor oil.

My childhood was steeped in automobile culture, so as a young man I was disheartened to see the sudden decline of independent dealerships. I watched as mega-dealerships came in and wiped out one small dealership after the next, but I didn't know exactly why that had happened until I began working on my thesis.

I did my fair share of traditional research, but when I conducted oral histories at dealerships that had been founded in 1920s, I was able to form a more complete picture of what was happening.

I learned firsthand about the difference between the way Henry Ford ruthlessly controlled his dealers and the way General Motors supported theirs. I learned about the changing economics of the agency system. The ever-shifting challenges of manufacturing overcapacity and scarcity. The financial risks to the dealer of Free on Board (FOB) delivery. As well as the importance of incentives clauses—disguised as "contests"—stacked in favor of the manufacturer.

In some ways, my thesis reinforced something I had already learned from my father. Facts and figures are important. Every organization needs a genealogy, but when you want to get at the meaning of events, you have to sit down with the people who actually lived through them.

It doesn't matter if an interview subject is an emotional, touchy-feely kind of person. Give someone the opportunity to recount pivotal moments in their career and you'll unearth some deep-seated feelings and insights. Sometimes, a good oral history session even acts as therapy, allowing individuals or entire organizations to exercise demons that have been haunting them for years.

In 1981, for example, I was commissioned to do my first official oral history project for a large financial institution. At the time, the company's legendary ex-chairman and CEO was looking for support in writing a history of his bank.

No one knew the bank better than the ex-chairman, but he had run into a roadblock that no one could quite understand.

I asked him to put together a list of interviewees to help me fill in some gaps in the bank's history when I discovered a skeleton in the closet.

As it turns out, the ex-chairman's handpicked successor had committed suicide, an act that had cast a pall over the bank and his successors. It haunted the ex-chairman, to the point where it was getting in the way of him properly telling the bank's story.

In doing some careful research and connecting everyone's oral histories, it became clear that it wasn't just the stress of the job that had driven that man to suicide. There were plenty of other factors, including the side effects of a new blood pressure medication he had been taking.

My oral history work proved to be liberating for the ex-chairman, who had been blaming himself for the tragedy. Thanks to our talks, he was now able to interpret the bank's history with enthusiasm and a personal touch that resulted in a meaningful publication.

Group oral histories can be just as cathartic, fueled by the rapid-fire exchange of people sitting in a room, sharing insights. When I conducted our first series of videotaped oral histories for the Greater Washington Board of Trade back in 1987, I gathered together small groups, which included a former mayor, business leaders and civil rights leaders, in order to share their experiences.

The discussions were organized around specific themes or epochs. One group was invited to talk about D.C. during the riots in the late 1960s; another group discussed the suburbanization of Virginia in the 1970s. And so on.

I guided the discussion and let everyone feed off each other's thoughts. You didn't see the institution through one perspective;

you saw it through multiple lenses at the same moment, which provided a depth of knowledge that was truly stunning. That project was so successful, in fact, that The George Washington University acquired the tapes for its own archive on the history of the nation's capital.

The Way Forward: VHS, Cassette Tapes and Call Centers

Our success in conducting group oral histories for the Greater Washington Board of Trade gave us the confidence in the late 1980s to begin taping individual oral histories, a technological innovation that added an extra layer of humanity to the process. From an interpretive perspective, you can glean a lot more from seeing someone talk about their lives than from simply reading words on a page. Transcripts don't pick up someone's tone of voice or facial expressions, which can speak volumes about an individual's personality, grit and overall charisma.

And yet I kept thinking about ways we might be able to broaden our oral histories to capture the stories and feelings of the boots-on-the-ground employees and managers whose stories never seemed to be captured and preserved. I knew that videotaping at that time would be a financial and logistical impossibility, but I felt the next best thing was to get audio of these people's stories.

My plan—an unheard-of concept at the time—was to mass-mail blank cassette tapes with a list of questions to employees so they could tell their own stories in their own words. This was back when oral histories were relatively unknown and Story Corps wasn't even a glimmer in its founder's eye—but we did it anyway. We sent out cassettes and found that everyday employees appreciated having their voices heard and seeing their stories in print.

Then, during a chance encounter in the early 1990s, I met someone who was responsible for setting up large call centers for big companies across the country, and that got me thinking. Call center operators are used to working with scripts. Usually they're responding to sales inquiries, but what if those same call center operators were prompted to record inbound callers' stories instead? What if we replaced sales scripts with a list of oral history questions?

One of our clients, International Paper, liked the idea, so we sent out letters to current and former employees with an 800 number they could call to share their stories. They'd dial, and someone at a call center halfway across the United States would pick up the phone and say, "Hello, International Paper Storyline."

That would start the conversation rolling. The line operators had prompts. *What's your name?* Marion Wilson. *OK, where do you live?* Biloxi, Mississippi. *OK, Marion, what years did you work for International Paper?* I worked there from 1962 to 1989. *Marion, let me ask you a question: What was it like joining International Paper in 1962?*

And on it went. We'd have the line operators tag each call with details about the stories being told and the years that were discussed. And then this information was formulated into a printout at the end of every day. We knew which stories we had and which ones we were missing during every stage of the process, and then sent out new requests to fill in the gaps.

The technology required to digitally leverage the audio files wasn't economically feasible, so we converted them into an analog format in a book called *Generations of Pride*, which told the story of International Paper from multiple perspectives, from the bottom of the company all the way up to the top.

In the back of the book, we included the name of every person who called in, which helped give the employees of International Paper a sense of ownership over the history of their company.

Growth Meets Crisis:
The Oral Histories of Accenture and Arthur Andersen

In the years ahead, I continued to venture around the world conducting oral histories. I was interviewing groups and individuals, using handheld video cameras and digital recording devices. But there are few oral history projects more illuminating than the ones we conducted for Arthur Andersen and Accenture.

In the late 1980s, we were engaged by Arthur Andersen to conduct a series of oral histories to capture the firm's unwritten history. One of the interview subjects, Harvey Kapnick, was a former managing partner who had warned his fellow partners of the inherent conflicts of interest that could arise from consultants and accountants working for the same clients. Harvey's proposed solution—separating the firm's rapidly growing Management Information Consulting Division (MICD) from Arthur Andersen's plodding auditing division—was met with such overwhelming resistance from the partners that he was forced to resign. It probably didn't help Harvey's cause that he let it be known that he planned to abandon the accountants and join the consultants after the proposed split.

In time, MICD grew to the point where it was almost equal in size to its parent company. By 1989, the writing was on the wall. MICD was in an unregulated industry; Arthur Andersen was in a deeply regulated one. MICD was in the technology field; Arthur Andersen was in the accounting field. MICD was minting money. Arthur Andersen's fees had flatlined.

You can see where this is going: The grown child was ready to leave the roost and strike out on its own. And thus in 1989, Arthur Andersen and Andersen Consulting became separate units. But the quality of our work documenting the lives and careers of Arthur Andersen executives made an impression on the consulting wing of the company, Andersen Consulting, which decided to commission its own set of oral histories in 1992.

So I got out my passport and embarked on a second globe-trotting adventure, this time interviewing a large swath of Andersen Consulting's leaders. There was one key difference between the two projects. At Arthur, I had interviewed all of the managing partners, many of whom were looking back at Arthur Andersen's golden age. At Andersen Consulting, I interviewed the young, innovative leaders who saw a bright new future.

Anderson Consulting was—to borrow a History Factory maxim—an example of our Start with the Future and Work Back methodology in action. Andersen Consulting used its oral histories as motivation to keep moving forward, gaining more self-determination every day.

That didn't surprise me at all. Oral histories have always been great motivating tools. Our oral history work with Andersen Consulting gave the company a history it could build on. Meanwhile, my original oral histories with Arthur Andersen had the opposite effect. Although I didn't realize it at the time, I was documenting, in real time, an organization headed in the opposite direction.

We all know what happened next. Enron blew up. Papers

were shredded. The FBI came calling and Arthur Andersen became a memory.

By contrast, Andersen Consulting continued to flourish. The company changed its name to Accenture in 2001 and decided to go public that same year. A few years later, I received a call from the company's communications department, which wanted us to document the end of the company's partnership with Arthur Andersen and record what it had achieved in the years since the split.

We were commissioned to conduct more oral histories, reorganize Accenture's archives and write a book, which the company planned to give to 300 former partners in recognition of their contributions in building the firm.

As the book neared completion, however, excitement began to build. When early reviewers within Accenture began reading it, everyone echoed the same compliment. "After reading this book," they said, "we feel proud of ourselves and our company."

And when Accenture's new CEO, William Green, took a look at it, he asked his communications team how many copies they planned to print.

When the team informed him that a 300-copy run was planned, Green turned to them with a surprised look on his face and asked how much each book cost to produce. When the answer came back at around $40 each, he said, "It costs more than that to take a new employee out to lunch. I want to give a copy of this book to every single one of our employees."

Within an instant, the print run grew from 300 to 110,000.

We still have pictures of a convoy of tractor trailers filled with paper arriving for the print run. And as an added bonus, each book came with a CD titled "The People Behind the Accenture Story," which included many of the videotaped oral histories I had conducted more than a decade earlier.

In the end, Arthur Andersen had hired The History Factory to document what it had already achieved, while Accenture used the past to launch itself toward a more ambitious future. And thus the story of Arthur Andersen and Accenture provides evidence that what you glean from an oral history project matters, but what you choose to do with those findings matters even more.

The Dawn of Discover: The Democratization of Oral Histories

Nothing will get a group of employees more engaged or emotionally connected to an organization than listening to a past leader who has taken the time to leave a record of his or her insights and motivations.

Think about McDonald's. There are a billion Ray Kroc stories, and they all have a moral. Some are about quality, some are about competitiveness, but all are designed to make you feel more connected to the man and his restaurants.

Oral histories provide these types of stories. Every organization has a founder. They all have a creation story. It doesn't matter that the Boeing Corporation left its headquarters in Seattle for Chicago. The company still talks about founder Bill Boeing and his days in the Emerald City. They still quote him. They still talk about his pioneering insights into flight and how he helped usher in a golden age of aviation. The character and story of Bill Boeing has continued to resonate long after his death. Think of it this way: An organization's founder is its creation story molded into human form.

But everyone likes a good unsung hero as well. The guy in the next cubicle who went above and beyond his pay grade. The middle manager who cared. The scientist, banker or salesman who symbolized the very soul of the organization. We're all looking for someone to relate to—people who become symbols of what an entire organization is and stands for.

Because everyday employees have great value, I often encourage clients to conduct oral histories throughout the ranks of their organization. Collecting stories from the rank and file can make everyone in your organization feel connected to the company in deep and meaningful ways.

After all, employees' experiences tend to be shaped by where they are on the hierarchy. It's like being on a giant ocean liner. The CEOs are on the top deck and they can see the tremendous expanse of potential growth ahead. But almost everyone else is below deck. They can't see what's going on. They want to know where the boat is headed. What's the course? How do the waves look? What's the next port of call? But they're all down in their cabins—essentially in the dark—so they don't have a clear sense of the overall direction of the organization.

Stories, and the oral histories that give birth to them, provide employees with a view that's well beyond where they are in the organization. Stories help define the experience for them. Oral histories give everyone a view from the deck, which pushes them to do more.

Our work with Discover in 2010 provides a perfect example of that principle in action.

The truth of the matter is that we'd worked with a number of clients who had played a role in the Discover story, including

Sears, which launched Discover in 1985. Thanks to our extensive work with the banking industry, we had a thorough understanding of the history of the credit card industry. Plus, I had conducted an oral history with Ed Telling, the Sears CEO who gave birth to the idea of Discover in the 1980s.

So when we showed up to our meeting, I was peeling off Discover stories like I had worked there for 25 years. It would be like me showing up at someone's house and saying, "You know, your grandfather used to ride the L train and eat lunch every day at the Corner Grill."

During the meeting, the Discover people kept turning to me and asking, "Wait. How did you know that?" And we quickly won the privilege of working on Discover's 25th anniversary celebration.

At the time, the financial services industry was being demonized as one of the chief instigators of the 2008 mortgage crisis. The pitchforks were out. It didn't matter what you did: If you worked in the financial services industry, you were the enemy.

Discover's company officials confessed that they had an additional problem. The Discover card was being portrayed as the cheap, goofy stepchild of the credit card industry, and they wanted to put an end to that misrepresentation. It was beginning to affect morale, in part because so many new Discover employees simply didn't understand the history of their own company.

We knew we could change that. And we did. One of the advantages of working with a 25-year-old company is that you still have the ability to conduct oral histories with its founders. In the case of Discover, these early employees were referred to as "the Dawners," named after the "Dawn of Discover" television ads that launched the card during Super Bowl XX.

When the card launched in early 1986, there was a serious anti-Sears bias afoot. Merchants, especially independent sellers of washing machines and appliances, wouldn't accept the Discover card because they feared that it would help Sears, their deep-pocketed corporate rival. So it was a huge uphill battle, with opposition coming not only from merchants but also from an entrenched banking industry.

And yet, as the Dawners reminded us, the Discover card was unlike any other card on the market: a credit card that provided people with cash back on all their purchases. Today, you can find cash-back cards anywhere, but in the mid-1980s it was a rarity. Ultimately, it was Discover's appeal to consumers that propelled its growth.

And then came years of antitrust litigation, spurred by MasterCard and Visa. Year after year, Discover charged head-first into some extraordinary battles and won virtually every one of them. It was a great story that Discover's new employees simply didn't know.

How did we get those stories? By conducting a massive number of individual and group oral histories with people up and down the chain of command. We talked to Discover employees from coast to coast: people in sales, at call centers, and in development.

Meanwhile, the company conducted a series of employee surveys that gauged baseline attitudes and engagement, hoping to see if our work had an impact on morale. It certainly did. Over the course of the company's 25th anniversary year, we rolled out a series of short digital stories and documentary videos based on our archival research and all of the oral histories we had conducted. Biweekly multiple-choice history quizzes and quarterly anniversary sections followed, as well as an e-publication highlighting the culture of Discover that was based on employee responses to questions.

When the anniversary year ended, Discover monitored its employee engagement and concluded that the program was an unmitigated success. Some 9,000 of the company's 11,000 employees participated in its anniversary events. Surveys also revealed that 80 percent of respondents felt increased enthusiasm about working for Discover, while 88 percent felt that the anniversary recaptured the spark and spirit that people felt at Discover's inception.

All of this newfound confidence—this good will and excitement over the future—was simply a product of taking the time to listen to and communicate the experiences and feelings of the entire organization.

It all comes back to the democratization of content. Employees used to go looking for direction exclusively from those at the top. Now you see more and more organizations looking for its employees to inspire each other.

And how do you find the kinds of stories that bolster morale and become extraordinary motivational tools? You conduct oral histories.

Capture the right stories today and you can use them 10, 50 or 100 years from now.

SOLVING AN UNSOLVED MYSTERY: A TENNECO CASE STUDY

One of the best examples of how oral histories can solve a mystery involves our work in the 1990s with Tenneco, a pioneering conglomerate whose holdings ranged from a natural gas pipeline and farm implements to packaging and automotive parts.

We had been contracted to do some anniversary and oral history work, so I scheduled preliminary meetings with its leadership team to figure out whom I should begin interviewing. We began to create a list when a senior staff member cleared his throat and said, "Um, by the way. If you could find out why exactly why we acquired Newport News Shipping, could you let us know?"

That threw me for a bit of a loop. Newport News Shipping was one of the company's biggest divisions. I had assumed that the company possessed an in-depth understanding of why it had been acquired in the first place.

As it turned out, it didn't. When I asked the team what exactly they wanted to know, they informed me that the company's founder, Gardiner Symonds, had bought Newport News Shipping months before his death and never told anyone why he had made the acquisition.

One member of the team said, "To this day, we have no idea why we have it. We never figured out why Symonds wanted to add shipbuilding to our portfolio."

By conducting oral histories with people who had been at Tenneco during the acquisition, I found the answer.

During the 1960s, Tenneco was heavy into natural gas, a highly regulated industry. Around the same time, shipbuilding fell out of fashion, due to the winding down of the war and increased interest in different means of shipping.

The U.S. government believed that it was imperative that the country continue to have strong shipbuilding capabilities should we ever need to ramp up for another conflict. So it made a deal with Symonds: You purchase the shipyard and keep it afloat, and we'll make sure you have advantageous rates for your natural gas.

It was a classic quid pro quo, but Symonds obliged and the deal was done. Tenneco was in the shipping business.

When I returned to the leadership team and reported what I had found, they were grateful. They finally had an answer to a mystery that had been plaguing the company for years.

And in due time, they sold off Newport News Shipping, allowing the company to focus on what it did best instead of holding onto an acquisition that had long outgrown its usefulness.

4

SEEING IS BELIEVING

The Power of Corporate Exhibits and Organizational Icons

Some organizations are content to paper over their walls with generic and message-free corporate artwork. That's fine. That's their prerogative. But if all my time working in corporate heritage has taught me anything, it's that people gravitate toward authenticity more than artifice. They want the real. And when they find it, they connect with it on both an intellectual and visceral level.

Take, for instance, our work with HarperCollins. When we were contacted by the company in 2012, the leadership team made it clear that they wanted an exhibit that spoke directly to its authors—communicating, especially, the fact that Harper-Collins was committed to putting the needs and aspirations of its authors above all else in every decision it made.

Walking into a traditional publisher's office used to feel a little bit like taking a trip to the principal's office. Dark hallways. Dark wood. Dark offices. At times, you couldn't help but feel you were entering some little rabbit warren, where editors disappeared into their offices, red pen in hand, scribbling tirelessly away at big stacks of anonymous manuscripts. In other words, the kind of environment where it's easy to forget that the author is, and always has been, the most important part of the publishing process.

To counter this misconception, HarperCollins created a wide-open work space at its new headquarters in Lower Manhattan—a space positively brimming with light and transparency. On the one hand, it reminded authors that HarperCollins wasn't stuck in the past. And yet it didn't particularly communicate HarperCollins' own unique history as the publisher of choice for some of the world's greatest authors, from Charles Dickens and Mark Twain to Agatha Christie and Harper Lee.

We knew that the tone of our exhibit had to be aspirational. It had to make authors feel pride to be a part of the HarperCollins family. Fortunately, while doing our research we found a wonderful symbol of that very idea: a spiral wrought-iron staircase in one of its earliest headquarters buildings that a veritable pantheon of legendary writers had ascended over the years.

We found a magnificently telling quote that said, "They join us as unknowns and leave us as knowns."

That was the central message HarperCollins wanted to communicate—namely, that authors are important to us. We nurture them. We turn unknowns into literary giants.

So we did something rather ambitious. As the centerpiece for a headquarters-wide exhibit program, we built a massive "author bookcase" to flank the new space's dramatic two-story staircase and filled it with stories, quotes, pictures and artifacts from some of HarperCollins' most famous authors.

The bookcase was mapped out intentionally. On the left, it profiled the early trials of each author—whether they were personal difficulties or their struggles getting published by other houses. And then as viewers moved along the wall, each vignette revealed how HarperCollins had supported these writers on their path toward literary immortality, ending with segments from published books and subsequent work on the right.

We started with early submissions on one side and ended with success and acclaim on the other. And the bridge between those two extremes was HarperCollins.

HarperCollins CEO Brian Murray has gone on the record as saying that the exhibit not only changed the way authors perceive the company but also the way HarperCollins thinks about itself.

Now, whenever HarperCollins editors look up at our exhibit, they are reminded—day in and day out—of the fine work that their predecessors did as well as the fact that the manuscript they are currently working on may belong to the next Zora Neale Hurston or Maurice Sendak.

When writers walk into HarperCollins' headquarters, they see the names and stories of illustrious authors on the wall and they feel as if they've entered the pantheon of the literary world. Everyone, whether they're a budding author or an established one, looks up and says the same thing. "I want to be part of that group. I want to be on that wall."

Home Is Where the Heart Is: Building Exhibits in Corporate Spaces

At The History Factory, we build corporate exhibits in order to tell a story in three dimensions. They're constructed in layers. We start by asking basic questions. What's the story that we have to tell? Who are the characters at the center of that story? What's the tone? What materials do we want to use? And what's the space we have to work with?

And we take the time needed to fully consider how a particular exhibit can provide our clients with real-world value. Do we want to boost employee engagement, change public perception of our client, or meet some other goal that is on the company's wish list?

Great exhibits, therefore, are designed to inform. When all is said and done, they change the way an organization is viewed from the outside (clients, media, potential hires and the general public) as well as the inside (each and every individual up and down the corporate ladder).

Over the years, our clients have asked us to mount corporate exhibits for a variety of reasons. But in my experience, exhibit creation tends to be motivated by one thing: pride.

Great companies accomplish great things. And inevitably there comes a time when an organization takes a moment to look at what it has achieved and starts saying, "More people need to know about all of this. Why are we keeping it a secret? Why don't we start showing everyone who we are and all that we've done?"

We've produced a number of traveling exhibits over the years, but the majority of our installations are housed in the offices, work spaces and factories where people work. Why? Because telling potential clients or new hires what you've accomplished is one thing; showing them in your own space is another thing altogether.

Just think about your own home for a moment. After the initial exchange of pleasantries, what do people tend to do when they come over to your home? At our house, people immediately look at the bookshelf, which is located right next to the front entrance.

"Oh, you're interested in history?" people say. "Music? Business? Biography? Me, too." And then people invariably walk over to our side table and look at pictures of our family, which provides a different sense of trust and comfort.

All the things in my home, taken together, make a statement about me and my wife, Susan, and what's important to us, just as a corporate exhibit does. So why should it be any different for the home of your particular organization?

Objects of Historical Beauty

Over the years, we've produced corporate exhibits for a wide range of clients from Boston Scientific to Pella to UniGroup—displays of every shape and size that have filled just about every type of corporate office, board room and lobby you can imagine.

During the early 1980s, however, back when The History Factory was in its infancy, very few organizations gave much thought to corporate exhibits. They were considered luxuries, as opposed to what they really are: relatively inexpensive capital investments that generate a great deal of long-term value.

During the early '80s, most organizations were busy selling as much real estate as possible just to stay afloat, which left us with very little space—and even fewer opportunities—to show what we could do.

You could hardly blame them. Most corporate exhibits back then were painfully old-fashioned. Exhibit creators tended to do one of two things: build a diorama of a famous office space or dress up a few mannequins to look like famous company leaders.

Everyone seemed to be in a competition to see who could do the best Madame Tussauds impression, completely ignoring the responsibility to build corporate exhibits that provided a good return on investment.

In the museum world, however, there was a concerted effort to move away from that kind of faux realism toward more representational exhibits. Go visit a maritime exhibit at the Smithsonian and you might find a beautiful tapestry of rope made entirely out of different sailors' knots.

Visit the John F. Kennedy Presidential Library and you wouldn't find JFK's desk sitting in a staged re-creation of the Oval Office; you'd find it carefully positioned on a platform in the middle of a dark room, illuminated by a single spotlight shining down from the rafters.

You could go stand in front of that desk and let your imagination run wild. The idea wasn't to tell people too much about the object or distract them with a busy backdrop. The goal was to use a physical object—a real artifact—to tell a story and invoke a sense of wonder.

When you walked into JFK's library and stood in front of his desk, you couldn't help but say to yourself, "Wow. I get it now. I can imagine what it must have been like to sit in that desk, alone in the dark, during the Cuban Missile Crisis."

That's what I wanted to bring to corporate America. I wanted to transform business artifacts into thought-provoking works of art. I wanted to tell stories in new ways. I wanted to create exhibits that generated media attention. And above all, I wanted to prove, once and for all, that a properly produced corporate exhibit could be every bit as compelling as one dedicated to politics or the natural world.

In my opinion, that's what great corporate exhibits are. They are wonderful little walled cities that manage to entertain while they inform. They are three-dimensional documentaries that pull together words, images, colors and physical objects in a way that makes others understand the values, culture and achievements of great organizations.

The only question I had, back in the early '80s, was whether anyone would ever give me a chance to prove that it could be done.

Lobbying for Change at Bank of Bethesda

Archivists are experts at cataloging an organization's artifacts, but our creatives are often the ones who decide what has value and what doesn't.

I've known this from day one, which is why The History Factory has always employed writers, designers and exhibit creators to work alongside archivists during the planning phase of each project.

Finding the right artifacts to use in an exhibit isn't so much about the object itself as it is about the meaning and symbolism that the object can communicate.

In the early 1980s, banks, which had recently been deregulated, started to recognize the importance of financial literature—those now-ubiquitous brochures you find in every bank lobby. Financial institutions made it known that they were looking for innovative ways to showcase these booklets to customers.

I knew that the cost of custom-made cabinetry was becoming prohibitively expensive, so I visited banks around Washington, D.C., and pitched the idea of lobby-based corporate exhibits.

Representatives for Bank of Bethesda liked my ideas but confessed they were having a difficult time livening up the lobby of one of their rather dreary-looking branches.

Dreary may be an understatement. The bank looked like a fully preserved World War II bunker. We're talking true brutalist architecture—a poured concrete pillbox of a building that sat despondently in the middle of a suburban shopping-center parking lot.

If you drove by it, you'd have no clue it was a bank, let alone a branch of Bank of Bethesda, which was known for its architecturally rich headquarters building perched at the junction of Wisconsin Avenue and Old Georgetown Road. The headquarters building was a suburban Washington, D.C., landmark.

Once you walked inside, things got worse. Its lobby was so soulless and sterile that most people wanted to leave before they finished depositing their checks.

Company executives grumbled that they didn't want to spend the money needed to decorate the room with corporate artwork.

I, of course, insisted that they didn't have to.

I told them that if they let me delve into their archives, I'd be able to produce a lobby exhibit for a fraction of what a shipment of high-priced corporate artwork might cost.

And I did just that. In the basement of the bank's headquarters, I unearthed plenty of eye-catching maps, letters, and black-and-white photographs. My most important discovery of all, however, was an old ledger book dating back to the bank's first day in operation in 1919, which I quickly set aside to be the centerpiece for the entire exhibit.

I wanted to be subtle. I knew that Bank of Bethesda customers didn't want to be overwhelmed with large panels of text, so I opened the ledger book to its first page, slipped it into a sleek glass case that matched the room's décor and then camouflaged other historical *objets d'art* around the room.

None of the pieces called attention to themselves, especially the case with the ledger book inside. You could stand right next to it while writing a check and not even realize it was there. But people who did spot it would stop in their tracks, crane their neck down, and begin carefully reading the page.

That's when you'd see their eyebrows begin to rise and they'd begin to mutter things under their breath, like "hmmm," "interesting" and "that's cool," before walking over to the teller and asking whether that ledger book was, in fact, real. (Which, of course, it was.)

When you allow people to make discoveries on their own, they take ownership over a space. Everyone becomes an amateur tour guide. They started hauling in family members and pointing at things on the walls. "Did you see that over there? That's their first logo." Or "Look at that. It's a map of their first location from 70 years ago."

They felt like they had become members of a club, a part of Bank of Bethesda's story. And soon people forgot that they were standing in a soulless tomb. It simply became their bank. The one they knew. They one they trusted. The one they'd return to when they needed a second mortgage or a business loan.

After our work at Bank of Bethesda, other banks came calling, and the perceived value of lobby exhibits changed overnight. On a pure cost level, signing on with us was an undeniable bargain in 1980. A bank could pay $15,000 for a few fancy literature cases, or they could come to us and get a full exhibit for $10,000 that communicated a story of trust and the organization's core values.

Content Follows Architecture: Shell and the American Landscape

All of our early exhibits were successful. They got the word out for us, but I was sometimes frustrated that we were always being asked to build exhibits in tiny lobbies and closet-like spaces.

I had far grander plans for corporate exhibits than these spaces allowed and very few opportunities to showcase them.

Enter Shell Oil.

During the early 1980s, Texas enjoyed an extraordinary banking boom. Every major office building in the city had a bank branch in it. They were everywhere, acquiring valuable real estate across the region. And then, seemingly out of nowhere, they began rapidly disappearing thanks to the advent of the Texas banking crisis.

By the mid-1980s, Texas banks were failing at a rate unprecedented in U.S. history, leaving scores of office buildings with big empty spaces that needed to be filled.

This included the headquarters for Shell Oil, a company that soon found itself suffering through a unique identity crisis.

In order to understand Shell Oil's position at the time, you have to remember that it had been a majority-owned subsidiary of Royal Dutch Shell for decades. It was managed from Houston and listed on the New York Stock Exchange, and remained a U.S. company to offset the possibility of nationalization. During World War II, companies working in "vital industries," like Bayer and BASF, had been nationalized by the U.S. government, a threat that Dutch company leaders wanted to avoid at all costs.

By the 1980s, however, globalization had rendered the threat of corporate nationalization all but nil, and Royal Dutch Shell concluded it was safe to buy back 100 percent control of Shell Oil and delist it from NYSE in 1985.

It did just that, but not without huge ramifications.

Within weeks, a rival Houston-based oil company proclaimed itself the largest American oil company in Houston. A local hospital said it was the largest American employer in Houston. And yet another company boasted that it was the largest American contributor to the United Way in Houston.

Practically overnight, Shell Oil, which had a proud and compelling history in the United States, was branded a "foreign" company.

As a result, we received a call from Shell execs to come down and discuss an exhibit that would prove that Shell Oil, regardless of where its shareholders might live, was as American as apple pie.

The exhibit, which we purposefully titled "Shell and the American Landscape," occupied a cavernous space in the corporate headquarters lobby, which had been previously occupied by a now-shuttered Texas bank.

For the first time, we had a space large enough to match our ambitions. And fill it we did.

Shell executives made it clear that they didn't want any pictures of CEOs in their exhibit. Nothing corporate. No discussions of business strategies. They wanted an exhibit that told American history through the lens of Shell's many achievements.

So we brought in generations of gas pumps, a huge horse-drawn tank wagon, vivid artwork from old Shell gas stations, and amazing relics from aviator Jimmy Doolittle, who had been instrumental in Shell Oil's contribution to America's World War II effort with the development of 100-octane aviation fuel.

And it resonated. What surprised me more than anything was the number of visitors who had some kind of connection to Shell Oil.

We would bring school kids in—groups of 20—and at least three of each bunch would raise their hands and say that their uncle or dad had helped build floating platforms in the Gulf. And then another kid would invariably raise their hand and say that their uncle was working on that rig at that very moment. For people in Houston, it was an exhibit just as much about their lives and their ancestors as the company itself.

That's the key to any exhibit. You go, you experience it and then you feel compelled to take something with you when you leave. Build a great corporate exhibit, and some part of it lives on in people's memories long after they've left the building.

The success of our Shell exhibit changed everything. Not only did it draw crowds and plenty of media attention, it also proved that the benefits of a carefully planned corporate exhibit far outweighed the costs. To this day, Houstonians don't look at the iconic Shell Oil clamshell sign and think about the Dutch. They think and see Texas.

Heritage as Art: The Chrysler Makeover

It's always been important to me that we never pigeonhole ourselves into creating exhibits using any one strategy or approach. As we began to tinker with new technologies during the early 1990s, we found we could begin to vary the content and size of corporate images to evoke some very interesting ideas about our clients.

We began by helping our clients use their corporate logos in new ways. We'd weave, for example, pieces of information about the history of our clients inside their logo and then enlarge them so that the text was big enough to read. From afar, it just looked like a giant corporate symbol—a huge piece of wall art—but if you looked closer, you could see a trail of text winding through the curves of the logo.

In one sense, we were borrowing from the pop art movement. If Andy Warhol could turn a soup can into a piece of art, why couldn't we do the same with a corporate logo or an artifact? And from those early experiments came a new approach to corporate exhibits that we now refer to as our Heritage as Art program.

At the time, corporate office spaces themselves were becoming more decentralized. People were moving around a lot, so I felt as if we needed to democratize our approach to exhibits. And Chrysler gave us an opportunity to do just that.

During the late 1990s, the leadership in Chrysler's Washington, D.C., government affairs office came to us for an exhibit that highlighted—in a relatively subtle way—the automaker's commitment to innovation and quality. After flying out to Detroit, our team spent a day walking around the company's plants and offices. As a car guy, I was fascinated with the whole process. When we visited Chrysler's design lab, something sitting in the corner of the room caught my eye: It was a pile of what looked like giant turtle shells.

They were beautiful, all painted in an array of bright and bold colors. But when I picked a few up, they were surprisingly light. So light, in fact, that I knew they could be easily festooned to a wall.

I had no idea what they were until one of the designers told me that these forms were for testing paint. When engineers created new body designs, they needed to test how well the curved surfaces could hold primers and coatings, so they used these shells as paint testers.

That gave me an idea.

I asked if we could take a couple of them back to our offices. When we returned home, our team immediately started drawing up plans to hang these beautifully colored shells in some of Chrysler's conference rooms.

In my mind, these historical artifacts were nothing less than pieces of art. They were aesthetically stunning, sure, but they also were conversation starters. You could stand in front of these things and stare at them for hours. They were modern art that told a story and communicated core values. And thus our first Heritage as Art program was born.

When politicians, regulators, procurement officers or VIPs came in for a meeting at Chrysler's D.C. office and sat down in one of the company's conference rooms, almost without exception, they pointed up to the curved structures on the wall and said, "Those are really cool. What are they?"

From there, one conversation led to another. Company executives would begin talking about the Chrysler way—how each curve on every one of its cars had to be designed and then thoroughly tested to ensure durability and luster. That would then lead, naturally enough, to a discussion of Chrysler's "cab forward" design, which was one of the company's key differentiators at the time.

And thus what began as a corporate exhibit really turned into something else entirely. Every room in Chrysler's D.C. office became a lobbying tool, offering officials an opportunity to tell stories about Chrysler that they never would have been able to inconspicuously drop into a conversation otherwise.

Wayne's World: The Creation of a History Factory Icon

During the early 1990s, while we were busy pushing the envelope with our corporate exhibits, I made the decision to alter the look and feel of our own offices and corporate logos to match the work we were doing for our clients.

Back when we founded the Informative Design Group, my partner, Tom West, designed our company logo mark from three stylized block letters. It spelled out IDG by positioning a small letter "i" next to a capital D. When you looked closely inside that D, you could see a G carefully spiraled inside.

It had an Egyptian-esque, slightly Art Deco feel, as if it were a wood-block carving. It was geometric and distinctive, and it more than served its purpose. But when we moved into our new offices in Columbia Heights in 1989 and rebranded ourselves as The History Factory, I knew we needed to completely rethink our logo as well.

I'd always been attracted to the allegorical nature of old-fashioned stock certificates. Some were illustrated with vast Midwestern landscapes and others etched with everything from streetcars and grand old buildings to company leaders or revered historical figures. Regardless of what the specific drawings might have been, they all told a story. I wanted our logo to do that as well.

On the left of our logo, I wanted to see illustrations of technologies and buildings from the past: an easel, an ionic column and an old scroll. And on the right, I wanted the tools and spaces we were working with at that time: a computer, floppy disks, skyscrapers, etc.

What we were missing, however, was something in the middle—some kind of symbol or character—to bridge that divide.

Fortunately, I had just conducted a series of oral history interviews with Dave Williams, then the CEO of Alliance Capital Management, who gave me a tour of his and his wife's impressive print collection. I was fascinated by it all, especially the propaganda art that featured heroic, hulking, square-jawed Russian factory workers who seemed to pop up on many Soviet posters.

I immediately told the design team I wanted them to add a big, burly worker in the center of our logo to underscore the "factory" in our name. So they added him, but he didn't look quite right.

We needed to soften him up a bit. So I asked them to make him look more like an American craftsman. And that helped. But I felt as if we were still missing something, so I asked my designers to draw a monocle over his right eye.

All the designers thought I'd gone crazy. "What? A monocle? That's going to look ridiculous," they said.

I said, "Just try it."

When the adjustments were made, I knew we had a winner. That logo exemplified who we were and what we were doing. You had the past and the present. A craftsman and a slightly quirky aristocrat. The look of a stock certificate and feel of a sophisticated illustration.

We named our mascot Wayne because the *Saturday Night Live* sketch "Wayne's World" was big at the time, and I was always asking our artists to give me more stuff in the background. "Give Wayne a world to live in," I'd say. And the name stuck.

At the time, everyone said "You're Wayne, aren't you?" And I'd tell them the truth. "I don't look like Wayne, but I'm Wayne in spirit." And I still am.

The logo also captured the look and feel of our offices at that time, which were packed full of archives, littered with quirky, creative people and absolutely brimming with energy.

My office, for instance, was located in an old wooden freight elevator. In order to find me, you had to go down to the stacks, walk through this dark archival area, and then look for a strange, glowing elevator shaft. I felt like the Wizard of Oz down there, tinkering with all these new ideas about how to build better exhibits and how to create unique new corporate anniversary programs.

Our logo captured the spirit of those days. There was a party nearly every night on the roof. It was young. It was cool. It was fun. And clients enjoyed visiting us. But then as our archival work expanded and the demand for new exhibits and books increased, we outgrew the space. We moved out to our vast new facility in Chantilly in 1995.

Times were changing, and we had to evolve and grow up

a bit to meet the needs of our expanding client base. All the big companies around Washington, D.C., were moving out near Dulles International Airport at that time, so we followed suit.

It really was a beautiful building. And it made a wonderful first impression. We'd pick up clients at the airport, drive them down this beautiful manicured corporate driveway and then turn a corner and there we were: this sprawling, brand-new development with "The History Factory" plastered across its façade in big, bold letters.

The look and feel of an organization's physical space matters a great deal. Don't let anyone tell you otherwise. It wasn't a perfect location. I missed a lot of the energy and the overall creative vibe that we had in Columbia Heights, but our move to Chantilly transformed us into a real business.

I used to joke that for the first 10 years of existence, we got paid out of the CEO's golf ball fund. And then when we became The History Factory and gained more visibility, we immediately moved toward the guys who had to make money—toward sales, advertising and marketing. No more ego trips for the boss. Our services became a more established and valued means of driving growth.

When we arrived at Chantilly, we became a full-fledged corporate heritage operation that could build multifaceted anniversary programs, create museum-worthy corporate exhibits and offer a level of archival services that would have put most universities to shame. Those were the places where there were bigger budgets and a higher perceived value. And our physical office space symbolized our readiness—and ability—to take on those new challenges.

The considerable reduction from D.C. office rents to suburban warehouse rents immediately went to the bottom line. The first year or two, we made good money. And with improved cash flow, we stopped relying on outside designers and handpicked our own team, which gave us the internal capability to meet our clients' needs, whether they be exhibits, videos, print products or online content.

In 1995, the software for network PCs began to stabilize, so we focused on internal and external networking. The evolution of Mosaic to Netscape fascinated me. The minute I saw browsers ignite the Internet, we began working on our own website.

In the beginning, our first site was slightly better than a print brochure. Then again, that's what everyone's website was like in 1995. Our mascot, Wayne, was the graphical element that anchored the whole thing, and we surrounded him with a variety of buttons that you could click to learn more about our services.

I remember being disappointed when I hired a creative team to try to loop some video into the site. They tried, but we just couldn't pull it off. They told me there wasn't enough bandwidth to make it work, so I pocketed that idea, hoping that one day in the not-too-distant future I could find a way to use an Internet-based video in one of our exhibits.

How to Build a Better Hologram

The Internet changed everything. During the late 1990s, new computer technologies transformed our approach to corporate exhibits by gravitating away from found artifacts toward interactive computer kiosks that could communicate an entire library worth of information with the press of a finger.

When we talk about the look and feel of an exhibit, we're not talking purely about design aesthetics. We're talking about the way a company talks about itself and how it tells its stories.

During the dot-com years, we took that sort of thinking to its logical extreme. Why transfer stories onto exhibit panels when we could digitally deliver them on demand?

When we worked with Andersen Consulting in the early 2000s, officials made it known that the medium was the message. They wanted their exhibit to highlight the firm's commitment to cutting-edge technology. Using artifacts just wouldn't do. I recalled having seen Pepsi's experiments with holograms in point-of-sale merchandising, so I decided to pitch the idea of creating a hologram to anchor the exhibit.

Andersen Consulting bought the idea. There were few precedents for holograms in corporate displays—or major museum exhibits, for that matter—but we found one of the leading hologram manufacturers in the United States to partner with us.

When guests walked into the Andersen Consulting exhibit, they were greeted by a hologram of CEO George Shaheen giving a speech about the values and culture of the firm. Surrounding the hologram was a series of interactive touch-screen kiosks that displayed an interactive timeline of the firm. Visitors could touch a date, and a video vignette would come on the screen and illustrate key Andersen Consulting engagements.

It blew people away. These weren't gimmicks. The hologram and the kiosks were used to underscore the fact that Andersen Consulting was a technologically leading firm that had its eye on the future—a mission statement that later motivated its split from its former parent company, Arthur Andersen.

The Andersen Consulting exhibit showed me that we were now freed from some of the physical constraints of traditional exhibits that we had struggled to overcome in the past.

During the 1980s and early 1990s, the amount of square footage we were given dictated what kind of exhibit we could mount. There's no way we could have created an exhibit on the scale of Shell and the American Landscape for one of our early banking clients. There simply wasn't enough room in their bank lobbies to pull it off.

Our work with Andersen Consulting, however, showed that we could distill an exhibit that should have taken up 15,000 square feet into a 30-foot by 30-foot space by using the right mix of technologies.

That was a breakthrough. From day one, our whole exhibit strategy has revolved around the changing nature of the workplace. In the early years, we called our projects "lobby exhibits" because lobbies were the only central place where people tended to congregate. That's where all the eyeballs were—in the lobby.

Up in a corporation's offices, you had a closed system, much like the publishing houses of old: long hallways, high-walled cubicles and plenty of offices where the doors were always shut.

When it comes to corporate exhibits, content always follows architecture. So when work spaces started to become more fluid and people began moving around a lot within those spaces, I pushed our clients toward Heritage as Art.

Instead of telling stories in a central location, Heritage as Art allowed us to decentralize messages, breaking up and redistributing them across multiple rooms and spaces, a move that mirrored the flow of corporate employees at that time.

In the years that followed, work spaces only became more fluid. Today, they're adhocracies through and through. You carry your desktop with you wherever you go. You sit down at a long computer table with a single monitor, plug in your laptop or tablet, go to work, and then disperse.

I can't help but feel we've come back to one of my original inspirations, the sociologist and architecture critic Lewis Mumford. Offices are now designed like mini cities. They have neighborhoods and circulation paths and a general openness that seeks to give people freedom in how they use space.

Those are the kinds of spaces we're designing into today. Not only are the offices moving, but the tools and laptops we need to do our jobs are mobile as well. So where do we put our corporate exhibits now?

The answer is: everywhere.

In some cases, our exhibits have been used to create landmarks. Recently, Weight Watchers hired us to create an exhibit format for an open floor plan. Things had gotten so open that we proposed using our exhibits as wayfinding devices, in much the same way that elevators in parking lots are thematically coded to help you recall where you parked your car. You've seen it before. Floor one is the Sinatra floor, with pictures of Old Blue Eyes by the elevators and one of his songs wafting through speakers. Floor two is B.B. King. Three is Benny Goodman, and so on.

For Weight Watchers, we decided to follow a similar approach. On the north side of its building, we told the history of Weight Watchers in the northern United States. On the south side of the building, we focused on stories from the South. And so on. So if you were looking at an exhibit panel describing the history of Birmingham, you were on 3-South. If it was talking about Minneapolis, it was 2-North.

The best part of these designs is that employees soak up the history of their company almost by osmosis. People will say, "I'll meet you in Founder's Square or Legacy Hall or the Minneapolis Room." And when they get there, what are they surrounded by? Content. History. Stories. Quotes. Images.

Pass by a powerful quote enough times and it'll stick. Not just the words, but the tone. The word choice. The intent. And the meaning. When we conduct oral histories now, they don't get sealed away in an archive only to be polished up and redisplayed every few years; they are built into the physical office space where employees and clients collaborate.

Because they are immersed in these content-rich spaces, employees now know—and are able to communicate—the history of their company with absolute confidence and purpose.

What we've done with exhibits for Weight Watchers and HarperCollins is change the way employees perceive themselves in relation to the organizations they work for. That's a great return on investment, which is the very thing I've been intent on proving since founding The History Factory.

Building Material Wealth: Hoffer and New Balance

Everything is cyclical. In recent years, as mobile technologies have become ubiquitous and on-demand text and video have become commonplace, our exhibits have found a better balance between the digital and the physical.

When we employ cutting-edge technologies in exhibits today, what we're really doing is providing opportunities for greater depth and accessibility, as well as the ability for visitors to go as deep into an organization's story as their time and interest level allow.

We can now provide visitors with the opportunity to download content they can take with them when they leave an exhibit or use their smartphones as surrogate tour guides. Mobile technologies allow us to inform and motivate in more dynamic ways, while the objects we display can convey a sense of history and emotion through the physical act of feeling and touching them.

Today, we have a broad palette of new materials to work with that were simply unavailable to us a few years ago. Take, for instance, our work with Hoffer Plastics, an industry leader in the field of injection moldings, a process that allows engineers to heat and then cool various materials into customized shapes using special molds. Today, injection-molding techniques are the basis for everything from bottle caps to auto parts.

If you want to know what kind of products Hoffer makes, just go to the company's exhibit and you can see them. The materials that we used to create Hoffer's exhibits are made from the very same materials that Hoffer uses in its own factories. You don't need to look at them through the distorted lens of a touch screen or a monitor. The exhibit shows you in three dimensions what the company is capable of doing.

To me, that's new and exciting. It's not so much that an exhibit is merely "about" something anymore; now, an exhibit actually is something, physically. In three dimensions.

We're crafting our exhibits out of the materials that our clients produce, quite literally out of who they are and what they're made of.

Look at our work with New Balance. Like so many forward-looking companies, New Balance has embraced the idea that an organization's physical space must convey its culture. The company's amazing new corporate headquarters boasts a soaring three-story atrium that invites in so much sunshine you can't help but want to take a stroll around the place—preferably in a comfortable pair of New Balance cross-trainers.

What the space needed, company officials told us, was a lobby-based experience that would showcase the history of New Balance products while offering visitors a glimpse of where the company was headed in the future.

It was music to my ears.

As we discovered more about the company's history, we learned that New Balance's founder, William J. Riley, came up with the idea for his company's famous arch support as a result of raising chickens in his backyard.

One day, while Riley was feeding his chickens, he noticed they had excellent balance, in part because of their tripod-shaped claws. That got him thinking: Why not build a special arch support that mimics the pronged foot of a chicken?

That claw-shaped design—as well as the company's three core values—are important symbols for New Balance, so we designed a 30-foot-tall claw-shaped structure for the company's massive lobby, which included dozens of triangular panels that told the story of the company through the evolution of its products.

Company officials liked the idea, especially that we were going to make the ground-level panels highly tactile, composed of actual footwear and apparel, as well as artifacts from athletes and associates.

Using a large touch screen at ground level, visitors can explore and delve into the content above and around them. It is a truly immersive experience. They can go as deep into the history of New Balance as time allows. There is a wealth of content, but the viewer stays in control. And best of all, it's authentic; it's all historically accurate. It's proof that history doesn't have to look old. In fact, it can look quite new.

As I always say, build the right exhibit and your past can look an awful lot like your future.

HOW TO TELL YOUR OWN STORY—THE SUBARU WAY

On a practical level, corporate exhibits warm the hearts of facility managers because they are a lot less expensive than fine art and architecturally they can fill any space. But what they capture more than anything else is the voice and culture of a company.

When we produced an anniversary exhibit for Subaru in 2003, we pulled out important objects from the company's history and asked employees to comment on them. One particularly illuminating find was an ancient teletype machine, which turned out to hold a great deal of meaning to many people in the company, especially early employees.

Because Subaru of America was the upstart marketing organization for Fuji Heavy Industries, half a world away in Japan, production orders were delivered via teletype machines, often in the middle of the night because of time zone differences.

When we showed early employees one of those teletype machines, they immediately started spinning great yarns—including how everyone rushed over to the teletype machines first thing in the morning.

If there was a lot of paper on the floor, they knew the day was going to be rough. If there wasn't a lot of paper on the floor, they knew things were going to be relatively placid. In their minds, that little machine had real power.

And yet it was the creative and impassioned ways these men and women told these stories that spoke volumes about the youthful culture of Subaru. So we made the decision not to write our own captions but to let company employees tell their own stories in their own words.

Their comments set the tone for the entire exhibit, giving it the kind of authenticity we wouldn't have captured if we had written the exhibit copy ourselves. When early drafts of that copy were circulated around the company, contemporary leaders were amazed at what they were hearing. "Wow," they'd say. "We didn't know any of this."

Our early efforts were so successful that we started digging around for things like design drawings of concept cars that were never built. Soon, engineers, designers and even office staff members were talking about these designs. They told us what they liked about them, what they were missing, and why they never came to fruition. These were deep insights, not just from management but from employees across the company.

The best part is that the commentary kept coming in, even after the exhibit was complete. When people visited the exhibit and saw that we were interested in capturing insights from across the hierarchy, people started emailing both The History Factory and company leaders to fill in gaps and add greater detail.

It was proof that an exhibit can deliver value from within, while generating an equal amount of interest from the outside world as well.

And it was all a product of being authentic to the company's own story and employee perspective.

5

HOW TO TELL A MEANINGFUL STORY

Video, Online Narratives and Corporate
Heritage for the Digital Age and Beyond

I've always believed that video—produced in the right way, with the right intent—offers the most honest way to communicate history.

Forget the stunts and tricks. When it comes to video, I'm a purist. All of today's bells and whistles—the colorization, incessant fades and wipes, the awkward-looking "special effects"— might look cutting-edge today, but I can guarantee you that they're going to look downright laughable a few years from now.

When we create a video, we're looking to create something that will stand the test of time. With emotion and sincerity. And, above all, authenticity.

The viewer should feel something. I'm talking about that knot you feel in your stomach when you watch a craftsman tell a story about their career—their life's work—and you see their eyes begin to tear up and hear their voice quiver with pride.

That's powerful. That's what humanizes an organization. That's what builds camaraderie and fellowship. That's what can make two recently merged companies feel like they're one bonded family—or make a demoralized one transform slumping morale into newfound enthusiasm and excitement.

You can't extract those kinds of emotions from a typewritten transcript. It's impossible. Can you feel them in a well-written book? Sure. But books have a certain aura of exclusivity to them. Giving a physical book to someone has become an almost ceremonial act.

If you're interested in relationship-building, there's nothing better than physically handing a book to a client or employee. But if you're looking for the most efficient way to reach out to large groups of people, inside or outside of an organization, it's usually through Web-based channels.

The Web, after all, is built for video, imagery and short online stories—we call the latter "touchstones"—that can deliver a message with brevity and impact.

I know that most C-suite leaders aren't accustomed to thinking about how they can communicate the spirit and meaning behind what they do or create.

And yet, who doesn't want to believe, in one way or another, that what they do for a living has meaning? Early in my career, it often took a great deal of time for the concept of "meaning" to ever enter into a conversation in corporate America.

That's changed. Today, I see people, up and down the corporate ladder, looking for careers and organizations that will give meaning to their lives and their chosen professions.

A lot of baby boomer CEOs like myself grew up in the

late '60s and early '70s, at a time when everything was about "meaning" and "keeping it real." Fast forward to today's millennials, who are even more obsessed with authenticity and meaning than we were. They're the ultimate "feel of real" generation.

Just look at the clever language we've developed to talk about our respective career choices.

A private equity investor isn't a hedge fund manager anymore; they're a job creator.

A pharmaceutical company doesn't manufacture drugs; it helps heal the world's children.

This recent turn toward building our career narratives around meaning is a good thing—especially for The History Factory—because meaning, by its very nature, is dependent on authenticity. After all, how can you truly be meaningful without being authentic?

Consider, for a moment, the backstory of the Tin Man in L. Frank Baum's classic *The Wizard of Oz*.

Originally, the Tin Man was a woodsman who fell in love with the witch's housekeeper. But the witch didn't want to lose her maid, so she put a hex on his hatchet, which slowly and systematically kept cutting off parts of his body. Every time the Tin Man lost a piece of himself, he built another out of metal. And because he never got the girl—and felt so heartbroken—he figured he simply didn't have a heart.

In my opinion, most organizations, large and small, suffer from a strain of the Tin Man Syndrome. Over time, in battle after battle, they systematically have to build another piece of armor. And after a while, they don't think they have a heart anymore.

All we do at The History Factory, whether through a video or an exhibit or a website, is do exactly what they did in *The Wizard of Oz*.

We just reintroduce them to their history, and say, "Of course you have a heart; here's your heart." And they gain their confidence back.

Videos are great tools for communicating that kind of emotion, especially if you can avoid using too many tricks in the editing suite.

That's my overarching philosophy on video: Keep it real.

When we create a video, we go back to the source material—to the real images and the actual words. If we say that Fred Astaire wore a foulard tie as a belt, we'll find an image of Fred Astaire wearing a foulard tie around his waist and then find the exact words he used to describe why he did it.

Watch the video we produced for Brooks Brothers—the one narrated by George Plimpton—and you'll see what I mean. There are no doctored images in there, just carefully curated photographs of the attached-collar shirts that F. Scott Fitzgerald wore in the 1920s, the ready-made suit Clark Gable wore when he wed Sylvia Ashley, and the multicolored socks and white button-down shirts that Andy Warhol spent his first paycheck on.

You set those images to the rhythms of Plimpton's textured narration—a voice he once aptly described as "Eastern seaboard cosmopolitan"—and you begin to feel the history of Brooks Brothers. You feel the grandeur and cachet that comes with wearing a perfectly tailored Brooks Brothers suit.

There's meaning there, as James Baldwin would say, on the

lower frequencies—a story that's not so much about clothing as it is about fashion innovation, glamour and prestige.

The Triumph of the Unmentionables: Kimberly-Clark and Scott Paper
Sometimes, seeing is the only path toward believing.

Whenever someone asks me how much impact a single video can have on an organization, I point them toward the work we did with Kimberly-Clark in 1997, just a few years after the company acquired longtime rival Scott Paper.

Most mergers and acquisitions tend to be messy affairs, in part because they're rife with uncertainty. Who's going to keep their job and who's going to get a pink slip? What's the new hierarchy? Where's the office going to be tomorrow? And so on.

We've helped smooth out countless M&As over the years, so I know the drill. Usually, the two sides sit across from each other as if they're total strangers, even though they're in the same industry and have survived the same traumas.

"We don't understand anything about them," one side will say, while the other says, "They're completely different from us."

So we go back into their respective history and find points of commonality. We say, "We see you guys have a great story about the nightmare of going from punch cards to magnetic tape in 1956." And then suddenly the guys across the table say, "Yes! We did, too. We worked 80 hours a week for a month on that. Do you remember those days?"

And it goes from there. The odd couple becomes bosom buddies. But the Kimberly-Scott relationship was a unique case. When Scott was acquired in 1995, it was one seriously demoralized company.

It had been run for several tumultuous years by Al Dunlap, whose well-earned nickname, "Chainsaw Al," pretty much summed up what he'd done to the company. He sawed the company's heart out, drove it into the ground, and then sold it off to Kimberly-Clark.

When devising a plan for Kimberly-Clark's 125th anniversary, we needed to find a way to incorporate Scott's history in hopes of engaging a highly demoralized work force. Our researchers went to work and quickly realized that there was, in fact, a fascinating overlap between the two.

Both of these companies boasted an unparalleled track record of product innovation. They weren't just brand stewards; they were product category creators who had developed, out of whole cloth, an amazing suite of products that had changed the lives of everyday American consumers.

Scott had paper towels and toilet tissue; Kimberly-Clark had Kotex, Kleenex and Depends. What was interesting, from my perspective, was that all of these products were the unmentionables of the retail world.

What do you associate with these products?

Bathrooms? Germs? Runny noses? Not particularly glamorous images, and yet these products truly did revolutionize our lives.

When we looked back at the histories of these products, we found that they were all created using innovative, and in some cases revolutionary, processes. But then there was a second key step that led to their widespread acceptance. Both companies had to educate consumers on why and how to use them.

And how did they do that exactly? Through groundbreaking advertising campaigns.

It was the perfect hook for a video, especially because Kimberly-Clark kept telling us they wanted to tell a global story.

There's nothing people enjoy more than watching ads in different languages. So we unearthed great old commercials and used them in a video that highlighted the symmetry between these two organizations.

We used a famous ad from the United Kingdom in which a puppy grabs a roll of toilet paper and runs down the stairs. We had Manners the Butler, a miniature butler in a derby hat who starred in a series of 1950s commercials for Kleenex. And then there were those famous ads where the musician Harry James stuffs a Kleenex into his trumpet and can't blow through it because the tissues are so strong.

We engaged Mariette Hartley, who was famous for her work with Polaroid, as narrator. You didn't see her, but you heard that great voice of hers.

We called the 12-minute piece "How the World Knows Kimberly-Clark," and it quickly became the centerpiece for the company's 125th-anniversary celebrations around the world. It was translated into 11 languages and used everywhere. It was uploaded to the company's internal Web portal; it got chopped up into small pieces and used during meetings and speeches. It was also used by Kimberly-Clark's ad team for inspiration.

At the beginning of the project, the people from Kimberly-Clark didn't know about Scott, and the Scott people didn't know a thing about Kimberly-Clark. But at the end of our work, they not only knew each other's stories, they felt a shared pride in what each had achieved. Two stories became one and set a path for the company's continued dominance today.

The Cable TV Effect: Experiments in Universal Distribution

During the 1980s and early 1990s, creating video for global corporations was a major headache. Clients wanted universal distribution of a video, which was expected to reach every branch, office and employee around the world at the exact same time.

That was, as you can imagine, easier said than done. There were time zone issues and a tangle of copyright laws. You had to create VHS and Betamax versions. Then you needed to copy the video onto PAL tapes for Europe. We'd label hundreds of these tapes by hand and ship them overseas—to Japan and India and London—without any clue as to how they might be used.

Some satellite offices showed them on gigantic screens at gala events. Others screened them in lunchrooms on small monitors. Nothing was uniform. It was a complete mess.

I was always looking for a way to get our videos to be more universally distributed—in essence, to get more eyeballs on them—when I began to take interest in the massive growth of the cable industry during the mid-1990s.

In 1996, I gained entry into that world when I was hired by CNNfn, CNN's financial network, to be an in-house historian and commentator.

Every Friday, I went into CNNfn's New York or Washington studios and talked about the big business happenings of the week from a historical perspective. If a new product launched, I would talk about the lineage of that item. If two companies were merging, I'd discuss their respective histories. I covered everything from the application of military technology for commercial use to the history of corporate scandal in the United States.

As I immersed myself in the cable news process, it became clear to me that young cable networks of all stripes were in dire need of quality content. During the early days of MSNBC, for example, the network didn't have any programming on the weekends because it was so focused on the markets. It was virtually dead air on Saturdays and Sundays.

So when The History Factory was contracted by International Paper to create a video celebrating the company's 100th anniversary in 1998, we recommended that the company purchase a half-hour block of airtime for the video on MSNBC for two consecutive Saturday afternoons. That way if people missed it one weekend, they could watch it the next.

The show itself was edited like a television show. It had a message from the CEO, a smattering of history, and interviews with key leaders who tied together the company's prestigious past with its promising future.

What I liked about the idea was that anyone who wanted to watch the show could simply turn on the TV, and there it was.

We found that employees were so excited about it that they called up their friends and said, "Hey, my company is going to be on TV on Saturday; you should check it out."

Because the video was on TV—and available for public consumption—it gained instant credibility. And because people could watch it in their own living rooms, with their families, instead of being ordered to watch it within the confines of an office, it became a great success.

It had reach. It was a YouTube moment before YouTube existed.

And it proved to be a turning point in our use of video. We had once again unhinged ourselves from convention. We'd never been rooted in anything traditional, but the success of the MSNBC gamble further validated our philosophy, thus allowing us to take full advantage of the shift toward online storytelling that followed in the years ahead.

The Voice of the Employee: Prudential's "Power of a Story" Campaign

Sometimes, video is simply a tool, a means for an organization to accumulate content that can yield some other deliverable. Our work with Prudential on what we called "The Power of a Story" in 2000 is an excellent illustration of how video can be harnessed to capture the soul of an organization, especially while it's in the midst of dramatic sea change.

During the mid- to late 1990s, when the stock market was setting records on a daily basis, many insurance companies made the decision to refocus on pushing annuities instead of selling traditional life insurance.

Sales calls changed overnight. People would pick up the phone and find that their friendly insurance agent no longer wanted to sell them an insurance policy that provided for their family in case of death, but rather, a policy that guaranteed them a steady stream of income in retirement.

The move was a product of the times, the stock-obsessed go-go '90s. I don't think insurance companies were trying to mislead people, but there was a groundswell of anger over some of the promises that were being made about these annuities. When you get enough people angry, they start filing complaints with a state's attorney general. And because every attorney general wants to be the next governor, they inevitably start filing lawsuits.

Prudential got caught in the crosshairs, facing the prospect of paying billions of dollars in settlements. A shake-up was called for. Prudential fired its CEO and brought in a banker named Art Ryan, the first outsider to become the CEO of the company.

It was around that time that we got a call from Prudential's director of communication, asking us for some help. Ryan had decided to bring his wife with him as he embarked on a company-wide listening tour. So while Ryan was up at the podium giving speeches, his wife would be sitting with Prudential employees, wives and sales agents—who would bombard her with questions as to what was happening to the company.

Poor Patricia Ryan. All she could do was shrug her shoulders, be honest, and say, "I don't know. I'm just married to the man." But Mrs. Ryan, who was an empathetic soul, never shooed anyone away. She was easy to talk to—and she listened well—so people started telling her stories about Prudential and why the company was so important to them.

Mrs. Ryan wanted to help. She wanted to find a way to harness all those great stories to help her husband and the company pull through this rough patch. Prudential's communication team asked whether The History Factory had any advice on how to do that. And we said, "Sure. We'll go out with Mrs. Ryan, and we'll collect stories. We'll videotape people telling the story of Prudential in their own words."

So we put together the Power of a Story program. Mrs. Ryan went out on the road to play a role that seemed a cross between Oprah and a Southern revival preacher.

The company would throw these massive luncheons and invite people to join the new CEO and his wife. Art would introduce himself on the dais, and then Mrs. Ryan would stand up and say, "Let me tell you a story."

She was masterful. She had the poise of a first lady. She'd tell a story about herself or her husband. And then she'd turn to everyone and ask people to share stories among themselves. We put prompts on cards at all the tables to help guide the discussion. And after all the sharing took place, Mrs. Ryan invited each table to share its best story.

It was a combination town-hall meeting and group therapy session. Cameras were positioned to capture the storytellers. We invited people from all divisions of the company—including Prudential Realty, Prudential Insurance and Prudential Financial—so people who had never met before could feel a sense of connection with each other, which helped underscore the idea that all of these divisions were part of one culture and one company—"One Prudential."

These luncheons revealed a number of compelling stories. During an event in Dallas, a mature African American woman stood up and said:

> When I joined this company, I was the only one.
> I had just graduated high school, and for my first job,
> I used to have to take three different buses. To get to
> Prudential, I only had to take two, so I joined them.
> There was no one like me. I used to go into the
> lunchroom, and I'd eat my lunch alone. Sometimes I would
> go at the end of the day and want to talk to someone—and
> no one would talk to me.

We sat there watching her speak, our hearts sinking, and we all wanted to bury our heads in shame. And then she said, "Yes. I was the only one; I was 18 and all the other woman there were in their 60s. The age gap was terrible."

She masterfully delivered that line. And the whole place just melted.

It was unpredictable, but so raw and real that you got swept up in the drama of it all, in seeing the history of this company from all these different perspectives.

You never knew what to expect. It was reality TV in the best—and probably only positive—sense of the phrase.

One woman got up and said, "When my husband joined Prudential, he told our college-bound children, 'If you're ever driving through a town and your car breaks down, don't call a mechanic; call a Prudential agent. He'll take care of you. He'll give you money. You'll stay at his house. He'll have your car fixed. Trust me on that.'"

You heard stories from people who lived through the Depression and people who refused to sign their application because it asked for their color. One man said, "I took it all the way to the state supreme court because I didn't believe that was right. I wasn't going to sign that document and answer that question."

They were stories about everyday heroes, which underscored Prudential's culture. And we had it all on tape, ready to be cut together, but there was no easy means of distributing it to the public.

This was back in 1998, when online video was something of a novelty, so we had to use the video footage to create a book, which was filled with all these stories. It turned out to be a great book, but it wasn't as interesting as seeing those stories being told by the people who lived them.

Fortunately, the book did its job. It gave Art Ryan a platform to say, "See, I care. I know the stories. I'm not an outsider anymore. I'm an insider. I'm like you because I've heard your stories. I know your stories. I can tell your stories."

It allowed Prudential to change without losing its character, which is one of the best ways an organization, whether large or small, can use its history. Those stories became a rallying cry for unity. And the Prudential that emerged from those dark days was a stronger, more unified company than it had been before its struggles.

The Age of Icons: The Art of Web-Based Storytelling

Most people will tell you that the Internet changed the way we read and consume content. That our desire for shorter and more stylized approaches to storytelling is purely a product of the maturation of digital media.

The Web easily pushes video and shorter narratives, therefore, we've quickly accepted—and embraced—these new forms of storytelling as the norm.

That's true to a degree. Video, for example, was a true game-changer for us. In the early days, when we used film to capture oral histories, the bulk of our budget was always swallowed up by the cost of purchasing, developing and editing film. We often shied away from filming oral histories because it was just too expensive.

With video, we could afford to just let the cameras roll. We could capture people's facial expressions and body language and voice inflections when they told stories. When you sat down with a CEO and asked him about a rough patch, say, in the late

1970s, you could see him fidget in his chair and hear the tension in his voice.

"Ugh, 1978," he'd say, staring at the floor. "That was a tough year."

And thus, video gave us—as well as our clients—an opportunity to move away from writing institutional histories toward telling more personal ones.

In all honesty, I think the technological shift is only part of the explanation. There's no doubt that video, audio and online content have a unique ability to convey emotion—to distill a story down to its essence.

But such a theory doesn't explain why everyone is more obsessed with the meaning of their careers—and the character of their employers—than ever before. If you're curious when this turn toward meaning began, I can propose a hard date. Everything changed on a single day: September 11, 2001.

As far as I'm concerned, 9/11 was the institutional equivalent of the day that John F. Kennedy was shot. It's a universal moment that everyone remembers. A kind of milestone in our collective lives.

Everyone in the United States felt it, but many of our corporate clients actually lived it.

We had clients—Fireman's Fund and Zurich—who lost employees that morning. And we had clients in buildings right next door—literally—who walked home and never went back. They saw it all, up close and personal: the falling bodies, the towers going down, the rubble and then the darkness.

I was in a Vancouver hotel room preparing for the day's meetings, so it was about 6 a.m. my time when I received an email from a Wisconsin friend—great guy, typical Midwesterner—who emailed me with two puzzling questions, "What's going on out there?" and "How can I help?"

I didn't know what he was talking about, so I clicked on the TV, and it was all right there. The towers collapsing, the planes in the air, the Pentagon on fire. So I rang my wife in Washington, where my family and I live, and I asked, "Are you OK? Where are you?"

"What's wrong?" she replied.

"What do you mean what's wrong?" I asked. "Have you seen what's happening at the Pentagon?"

She had no idea what was going on because she had been at the grocery store the whole time.

So there I was stuck in Vancouver, stranded for a week, feeling totally disconnected with what was happening at home. I couldn't do much. I just started making phone calls to ensure everyone was OK.

But I remember getting a photo in my inbox of some of our people at The History Factory going to the roof of our Chantilly offices and unfurling a huge flag from the top of the building. I wish I could have been up there with them, but I was so proud of our people for doing that nonetheless.

Everything changed after that, especially the way people perceived the idea of history. Everyone knew what they were doing at that moment—in the days and weeks and months after 9/11—was not only important but would be remembered and judged for decades to come.

It was a transformational moment, not only for the American psyche but also for storytelling in general. Stories, espe-

cially those rooted in history, became more iconic than infor-
mational. More than ever, our clients wanted us to tell stories
that were timeless—that played with ideas, symbolism and
more touching concepts.

Take, for instance, the work we did immediately after
9/11 for New York Life, a New York-based insurance company that owned one of the most iconic skyscrapers in Manhattan. You can imagine how 9/11 had a profound effect on
everyone in that organization.

On a practical level, there was serious concern over the
safety of its building and its people. And on top of all that, there
was the very real concern that the damage inflicted by the
attacks might bring the company—or even the whole insurance industry—to its knees.

The leaders of New York Life knew that they had to act
quickly to get ahead of people's fears before they metastasized
into a frenzy.

They called us into their offices and told us that they wanted
us to produce a collection of short stories that would assure policyholders and the public that New York Life was sound, secure
and more than capable of withstanding whatever shocks might
be on the horizon.

After digging into New York Life's history, we returned
to the communications team and said, "This is what you were
built for. You're a mutual company. In times like these, it's
never been about the financials for this company; it's been
about the loss of life. It's been about the small modicum of
security that you've always given to those who lose the most
during tragedies like this."

So we quickly developed a pamphlet—which was also inserted into the company's annual report and used on its website—that highlighted key moments of resilience across its 150-year history. We dug down and found fascinating stories about how the company weathered the great challenges of the 19th and 20th centuries: economic downturns, natural catastrophes and several wars.

New York Life, to its credit, was one of our first clients to identify the need for a different kind of historical voice—a voice that was focused exclusively on calming fears and relieving anxieties.

So that's what we did. We put New York Life and the security of its life insurance policies in context with what was happening at the time. The message was simple: "This is what we've done since day one, and this is what we're going to do moving forward."

There was a sudden and dramatic turn toward stories about compassion and a thirst for stories about employees doing amazing things. They were very human stories—an attempt to redefine organizations not as cold institutions but rather as a collection of people trying to do the right thing.

That was a big shift. Before 9/11, corporations tended to take a very literal view of history. I can't tell you how many organizations used to come to us and say, "We were founded in 1921. Why don't we have an anniversary celebration where we ask everyone to dress up like they're living in 1921?"

It used to drive me crazy. Nobody wanted to think about how their past was actually paving a path toward their future. They wanted to look backward, instead of using history to peer forward.

Luckily, we got some help from the advertising world, especially after 9/11. Heritage brands like Cadillac and Jeep and Levi Strauss started using their histories to tell interesting stories.

"Look at that sleek open-top 1959 Cadillac Eldorado," the ads seemed to be saying, "with those shark-like tail fins and chrome-plated bumpers. That's the very definition of stylish."

Cadillac didn't create ads so that people looked at a car and said, "Oh, that's an Eldorado. That's a car that says the 1950s." These were ads that transformed Cadillac into a symbol, a metaphor for luxury, style and good old-fashioned freedom on the open roads of America.

Part of what fueled this change was the sheer amount of information that everyone could now access on the Internet. Corporate timelines used to be sealed away in books; now they were easily available online. If you were looking for a broad outline of a company's history, you could find it on Wikipedia.

The facts were all there, ripe for the taking, but it's the underlying interpretation of those facts—the underlying meaning and character of an organization's history—that remained elusive and open to debate.

So we began to adjust. We introduced what we called touchstone stories—short, Web-friendly pieces that told parables about a company's past.

They weren't newspaper pieces; they were more like short magazine stories, artfully told profiles that combined the literary stylings of a good novelist with the academic discipline of a good historian.

Touchstones, which we continue to write for clients across the world today, are narrative icons—quick, entertaining reads that impart a message about the character and culture of a company.

And it was our turn toward touchstone writing that allowed us to create what we refer to as story banks, catalogs of image-rich stories that allow our clients to highlight key moments, people and achievements from their past.

The typical structure of a story bank today looks much like what you'd find if you log on to Netflix. It has its own landing page, but from there visitors can click on different sections built around specific themes.

Netflix's library of movies is broken up into genres – romantic comedies, documentaries, sci-fi and so on. Click on one of those genres and you'll find an image and a short description of each movie choice. One or two more clicks and you're watching your movie.

Our story banks employ a similar template. They're intuitive, based in some way on the subject trees we use to build archives. Click on a tab that reads "culture" and you'll get a cluster of stories about an organization's culture. Click on the "people" tab, and you'll get stories about leaders or individuals who played a key role in the company's development. And so on.

One of the first story banks we created was for American Century Investments in 2002. American Century was in a tremendous growth mode at that time—shifting from a founder-driven to a management-driven culture—and it needed a way to communicate the company's vision and history to the massive number of new employees and shareholders that were coming aboard.

This was an internal-facing story bank, meaning that it was created for people within the company to read and use as they saw fit. It was divided into simple thematic sections: products, teamwork, growth, values and so on. Click on the values section and you'd get a short engaging story about how the company developed one of its key technologies.

One of the openings, for instance, read like this:

> While attending a mutual fund conference with his wife, [founder] James Stowers had more on his mind than attending seminars. Late in the evening, Stowers sat in his hotel room thinking about the mountains of programming that he needed to start writing. Then the idea struck. Afraid to wake his wife and turn on the light, he took his books and headed into the bathroom. There, in a burst of inspiration, he spent the entire night in his hotel bathroom programming code for a breakthrough computer system. . . .

The best thing about a story bank is that it can be used in different ways by everyone in an organization. A new employee can read that James Stowers story and walk away with a better sense of his company's founder. A communication team can adapt it for a presentation or meeting. And a marketing team can use it as the inspiration to launch a new advertising push.

As a matter of fact, American Century's ad team did just that, using our stories to create a series of ads built around striking photographs of everyday objects that were tied to the company's history.

The one that was inspired by the Stowers story offered a

large black-and-white photograph of a bathtub, with opening text that read: "In the proud tradition of inventors in garages and attics, we offer a bathtub."

It went on to take small pieces of that story and link up its founder to the cult of innovators—like Steve Jobs and Jeff Bezos—that were all in vogue at that time.

Story banks, it should be noted, aren't always internally facing. Should a client want to build an external-facing story bank, we can do that as well. We simply build a website, like we did for Edelman Financial Services or Lockheed Martin, that presents these stories in stylized ways, almost like a digital magazine, for the general public.

Link those stories up to a company's social media page and you can start to drive traffic, which can lead to anything from media attention to increased business or a new partnership.

That's the power of Web-based touchstones: They're stories with a strategic message that entertain while they inform. People read them. And when you can engage the public—and draw them into your world—anything is possible.

A Convergence Moment: Video Meets Paper

Our work with video content and digital narratives kept us in a perfect position, straddled between the tactile and the digital. Convergence became—and remains to this very day—the most complete way to leverage organizational history. The question to ask is simple: How can you link the tactile and the digital, a book and a website, an exhibit and a social media feed, and thus pull different demographics and audiences into your cocoon of content and history?

It's no longer a question of push or pull, but in finding the right mixture of the two—in aligning the correct content channel to the right strategic objective. The key is to lock down the meaning of the story you're trying to tell.

Just as we've started looking for creative ways to produce exhibits out of the very materials that our clients produce or the essence of what they represent, we've also become focused on linking the digital and the tactile in our storytelling.

Look, for example, at the cross-platform work we did for Time Warner Cable in 2011, at a time when the company found itself at a crossroads. On the one hand, the people who built the company, on the cable side of the business, were beginning to retire and their stories needed to be documented. But on the other hand, company leaders also didn't want to de-emphasize the younger but increasingly vital broadband side of their business either.

At the same time, Time Warner Cable decided to stay focused on its heritage of engineering and innovation rather than getting into the entertainment and media business. The company developed a brand strategy that retained the heritage of its eye-ear graphic identity because it symbolized Time Warner Cable's commitment to delivering content on multiple platforms.

Initially, the company's pioneers said they simply wanted a book. But after we learned more about their current environment, we recommended an approach that would engage employees in the process and exemplify Time Warner Cable's brand promise by delivering its story in a multiplatform campaign.

To gather the content we needed in order to tell their story, we created a communications program called the "Memory Zone" to gather stories at in-person events and via internal social media. With the book as the centerpiece, we then developed the multiplatform approach, which included traveling displays, a short video trailer and a microsite to complement the publication in both print and e-book formats.

Everything from the book's color scheme to its physical feel took cues from the digital realm, cleverly juxtaposing a traditional historical narrative with large cinematic images. Located in the margins of the book were QR codes, which allowed readers to access auxiliary content using their smartphones.

Alternatively, those who started at the website could download an electronic copy of the book to access the more formal history of the company.

To celebrate the book and website launch, more than 150 industry leaders as well as key current and former employees attended a party at the New York Public Library's Beaux-Arts landmark main branch. And within a month of the website's launch, the book had been downloaded more than 15,000 times.

We titled the program, appropriately enough, "Making Connections." Which is, of course, what all great video and online content does. It plays into our innate desire to find a meaningful connection between who we are and what we do. It's storytelling with purpose, which is the only storytelling you'll find that stands the test of time and never, ever goes out of style.

OUR PIXAR MOMENT: COMPUTER ANIMATION
AND THE SARA LEE CORPORATION

During the 1980s and early 1990s, it was prohibitively expensive to film an oral history interview, let alone capture enough footage to create a documentary.

Video was primarily a push medium. You pushed content toward a satellite or onto a big screen. Typically, a video would be screened at a big event, like an anniversary or an important shareholder meeting. You'd show it once—usually while half of the audience was talking over it—and that was the end of it.

But that didn't stop us from doing some very creative work anyway. In 1989, for instance, we created one of the first fully computer-animated corporate videos of its kind for the 50th anniversary of the Sara Lee Corporation.

Sara Lee wanted to do something futuristic that proved it was a corporation with its eyes on tomorrow. We came up with the idea of building a huge model of a futuristic city and showing how all of Sara Lee's products were being used in this immersive "Tomorrowland."

The twist, of course, was that we decided to build our city using computer-based 3-D modeling software, so that viewers could fly through the city, almost like they were on a magic carpet, gliding past everything from people using Kiwi shoe polish to women carrying Coach bags.

Sara Lee debuted the production at the Art Institute of Chicago, where the company was holding its annual meeting. People told me it was like being on an amusement park ride. The video was ultimately entered in a number of high-profile competitions, which helped solidify The History Factory's reputation as a firm that not only took creative risks but knew how to transform a typical corporate gathering into an event truly worth remembering.

6

THE POWER OF STORYARC

The Art of Turning Crisis into Opportunity

Take an X-ray of any great story—from the Bible and *Romeo and Juliet* to *Indiana Jones* and *Star Wars*—and you'll find they all share a similar architecture. Plot lines change. Settings vary. Unique conflicts arise. But they all work from the same general set of blueprints.

There's always a setup. You meet a group of characters. You get to know them—who they are and what they believe in. A crisis arises, which builds tension and high drama. And finally, there's some sort of resolution. A character reacts to the danger and emerges on the other side, either triumphant or feeling far wiser having faced it.

This three-act dramatic structure—with a setup, a conflict and a resolution—is as time-tested a formula for great storytelling as you'll ever find. The Ancient Greeks were using it 2,500 years ago, and the best books, plays and movies all employ some version of it to this very day.

We've been writing corporate histories with these conventions in mind since the inception of The History Factory in 1979. In fact, we launched the company precisely because no one at the time—and I do mean no one—was writing corporate histories in a way that captured the inherent drama embedded in the backstories of great organizations.

Barbarians at the Gate, Bryan Burrough and John Helyar's game-changer of a corporate history about RJR Nabisco, had yet to be written. Nor had a subsequent string of fascinating works about corporate America, including Bethany McLean's *Enron: The Smartest Guys in the Room* or Adam Lashinsky's *Inside Apple,* come on the scene and revealed just how riveting and powerful corporate storytelling could be.

So we went out and wrote our own page-turners about our clients' histories, carefully blending sound historical research, business acumen and proven literary techniques. The goal? Make readers feel a connection—personal, emotional or intellectual— to these great stories while helping our clients achieve concrete organizational goals along the way.

Over time, however, I'd become interested in taking what we do instinctually and finding a way to codify it into a fine-tuned methodology that our clients could more clearly see and understand.

In the fall of 2008, as the subprime mortgage crisis hit and the wheels of the economy began to fall off, I got my chance.

Look at a timeline of all the major innovations that we've developed at The History Factory—from our video services to our next-gen LuminARC archival database—and you'll see that every single one of them has occurred during a major economic downturn.

Give us a little extra time and a little spare capacity, and we're going to find a way to put it to work—in this case, pouring our time and energy into improving and concretizing our methodologies.

So I teamed up with two filmmakers—Adam Nemett and Christian D'Andrea—who were as obsessed with the architecture of great narratives as I was. And we locked ourselves in an office space in downtown D.C. to brainstorm the art of storytelling.

We called our little think tank the "Idea Engine." It was our version of Skunk Works, the secretive Lockheed Martin development facility where engineers were encouraged to test the boundaries of what was possible in aeronautics. During the Cold War, Lockheed Martin's Skunk Works developed the U-2 spy plane and the SR-71 Blackbird, the world's fastest manned aircraft.

And at the Idea Engine, we created our own secret weapon, an information-capturing and storytelling methodology we call StoryARC™.

History as High Drama

In layman's terms, StoryARC is a process that helps us make a client's corporate history as compelling as a great movie or novel.

Nothing is fabricated. We stay true to the events as they happened, but StoryARC allows us to make sure our corporate histories have a dramatic arc and real narrative teeth. It keep our stories relevant to their intended audience while ensuring we meet the specific organizational needs outlined by our clients.

StoryARC maintains the traditional three-act structure that is at the core of every great story—setup, conflict, resolution—but adds a series of critical "hinge points" that help move a story along in an interesting way: awareness, commitment, challenge, danger and rebirth.

These hinge points are universal story conventions. They're the reason you spend $15 to go to the movies on a Saturday night or buy a $35 bestseller from your local bookstore. But they are also particularly useful when chronicling the history of a business or organization.

Look at the history of any great corporation and you'll see the importance of all these hinges. Take Sherwin-Williams, for example. Here's a company, way back in the late 19th century, that took 14 years to perfect the first high-quality premixed paint produced in the United States. That's awareness—and commitment.

Follow that particular chapter in Sherwin-Williams' history and you see all sorts of challenges and dangers emerge. How do you market a premixed paint when everything else on the market is blended by hand? How do you prove its quality? And how do you get your newfangled paint into dealers' hands?

It proved to be an interesting story, in part because the uncertainty that Sherwin-Williams faced in the 19th century is the very same uncertainty that businesses feel today. The past and the present have a way of dissolving into each other when you tell a well-crafted story.

In the case of Sherwin-Williams, that initial moment of uncertainty and risk led to a triumphant moment when customers started to buy its paint and realized just how special it was. It lasted longer, it was more durable, and it was more vibrant than other paints. Sherwin-Williams ready-mixed paints became the industry standard.

What I've outlined above is a StoryARC for a single epoch in the company's history, one focusing on early innovations, but you can easily take our StoryARC structure and apply it to different aspects of Sherwin-Williams' story, perhaps the story of its advertising campaigns or the evolution of its management principles.

You can use StoryARC to map out the entire 150-year history of the company or leverage its architecture to tell the story in an exhibit or in short, discrete online stories.

I know because we employed StoryARC to create all of the above for Sherwin-Williams, in preparation for the company's 150th anniversary in 2016. We produced a traditional book and a wide array of digital narratives and content, all of which lean on our StoryARC architecture for support.

But StoryARC isn't just a structure; it's also a fact-finding process. In order to identify the most important characters and plot lines in the Sherwin-Williams story, we conducted a series of StoryARC sessions with a broad range of employees.

StoryARC sessions are, in essence, historical focus groups. We gather one group or multiple groups of people from an organization to hear how they tell their own story. What do our clients think is important about their history? How do they perceive their own culture? How do they speak to each other?

Everyone at Sherwin-Williams, for instance, kept referencing something called "10 by 10," which came up at a meeting in Florida. What's 10 by 10? If you're an outsider, you have no clue what that means. So we asked people more about it.

We learned about the company's 10 by 10 campaign, which was Sherwin-Williams' attempt to fuel growth in 10 key metrics by 2010.

The company's leaders initially had decided not to announce its goals to the team. Too much pressure, they thought. Let's just keep doing what we're doing. But then during an employee gathering that CEO Chris Connor held in Florida, an employee raised his hand and asked, "Hey, Chris, tell us about this 10 by 10 initiative. We're really excited about this. We really think it's a good idea."

As it turns out, everyone knew about the 10 by 10 campaign already. There was already excitement across the company's ranks. It took off from there; the whole company embraced it, up and down the organization. So we found out what we didn't know and filled in the details we were missing.

That's classic gap analysis, seeing what we have and what we need to get in order to tell a story in the most interesting and accurate way possible.

And thus StoryARC helps us calibrate with absolute precision the stories we want to tell. It's a process that ensures three things—that our aim is true, that our stories remain relevant, and that each and every project we take on provides clients with a strong return on their time and investment.

Currency, Grain Elevators and the History of Global Liquidity

Shortly after we developed StoryARC, I was at an Executives' Club of Chicago luncheon when I ran into an old friend, Bill Parke, director of corporate marketing and financial communications at CME Group. I asked him what was new at CME.

Truth be told, that was a bit of a softball question. When you're running the most important derivatives and futures exchange market on the planet, handling an average of 3 billion contracts worth about $1 quadrillion annually, there's always something interesting going on.

But Bill confided in me that CME was facing a rather unique challenge. After its merger with the Chicago Board of Trade in 2007 and acquisition of NYMEX Holdings Inc. and COMEX in 2008, CME was looking for ways to weave the collective histories of all its organizations into a single unified story.

Bill confessed that the project was proving more difficult than he'd expected. So I told him about StoryARC and how I thought it might help him craft a more cohesive story.

He was interested, and we were contracted to work on a few of his speeches. Before we could even get started, however, Bill's boss, Anita Liskey, heard about the idea and invited us to another meeting. She was so impressed with the ideas we were presenting that she asked us to build a series of stories as well.

Our StoryARC methodology worked brilliantly. We outlined some compelling story lines, all of which aligned perfectly with our three-act structure and our all-important hinge points. There was the story of global liquidity, which moved from the origins of banking in Babylonia all the way to the rebirth of global financial markets in the late 20th century.

Other narratives surveyed the individual history of CME and its acquisitions, the history of global exchanges, and the evolution of self-regulation.

When the CEO of CME, Craig Donohue, read our stories, he asked us if we might be able to do even more. He informed us that CME was in the midst of designing a new executive floor and wondered if we could tell these stories in three dimensions within the executive level's hallways and conference rooms.

It was a great idea, so we got to work. We knew, however, that we had to be subtle. The displays had to complement the elegance of the executive floor's design. It couldn't look like an exhibit; it had to look like sophisticated artwork. So we utilized a simple palette of colors and kept the number of exhibit locations relatively small.

If you walked into the conference room that explored the story of global trade, for instance, you'd see a piece of art created from different currencies. From afar, you'd say, "Oh, that's just a piece of cool artwork." But once you got closer you'd see the way we laid out the currencies and wrote about them in a way that told a discrete story.

Go down the hall and you'd spot what looked like an ancient wooden staff but was actually a grain probe: a long, sleek piece of wood that farmers used to push into a grain elevator to ensure there wasn't a fake floor in place.

You'd lift your eyes from this beautiful grain probe to the wall above and read a story about the history of commodities trading.

It was a perfect blend of Heritage as Art and StoryARC, and it proved so popular that visiting officials and CEOs began asking for a tour of the floor as if they had just walked into the Art Institute of Chicago.

CME's people quickly became docents of their own history. Visitors to CME's executive suite wanted to know more about all these wonderful pieces of art and their accompanying stories, so everyone at CME became junior historians.

CME's story rippled through the organization organically and effortlessly, in part because we had taken the time to create a series of interesting stories worthy not only of telling but also of adorning the walls of CME's executive space.

Facing the Dark Moments: History as Catharsis

I highlight the CME story because it shows the ease with which StoryARC can be adapted to any deliverable, whether it's a book, a speech, an exhibit, a leadership conference or Web copy. If you include the right mix of participants, use a sound narrative structure, and then collaborate in finding key events and characters in a company's history, you've got a story that can take any form.

But one of the other great benefits of StoryARC is its innate ability to help organizations analyze crisis points in their history.

It's easy for any organizations to write about their groundbreaking accomplishments and achievements. Their breakthrough products. Their visionary founder. Their blockbuster earnings report. Their heartwarming disaster relief efforts.

That's all good and all important, but you can't ignore the most perilous moments from your past either, whether it's a key product failure or a bad management decision.

Why? Because people will read your story the exact same way that adolescent boys look at a dictionary. They're going to look for the dirty parts first.

That's just human nature. The stories that you're worried are the most offensive are most often the exact stories that your people are going to be most intent on rooting out.

And if those rough patches are conspicuously absent, it's going to undermine the credibility of your entire story.

What you have to do is offer context for those danger points. Most of the time, people obsess over things they don't understand. Think about medicine and the Internet. People feel a pain somewhere in their body; they Google their symptoms and begin panicking, thinking they have some debilitating disease. They often misdiagnose what they have, buy some cure-all pill that's being hawked online and wind up having to go to the doctor anyway.

It's the same thing with corporate lore. Most of the time, people don't have context on why an organization did what it did, so they internalize the wrong takeaways.

I've been consistent on this point since the inception of The History Factory. I've always said that the single fastest way to obliterate the credibility of an organization's history is to ignore or, worse yet, whitewash the most difficult aspects of the story.

The Fireman's Fund Story: The Flag that Still Flies

More often than not, the crises that organizations are reluctant to discuss emerge from a mundane set of circumstances: the introduction of a new piece of regulation, a management change, an unexpected economic downturn, or the surprise onset of a natural disaster.

I often point to our long-standing work with Fireman's Fund Insurance Company—which has endured all of the above—to illustrate how taking the time to work through a previous crisis can act as a hedge against future ones.

Launched in San Francisco in 1863, Fireman's Fund made a name for itself by donating a portion of its profits to help disabled volunteer firemen, their widows and their children.

Unfortunately, volunteer fire forces dwindled in urban areas in the latter half of the 19th century, transforming into the municipally controlled fire departments we know today.

Even though there were no longer any volunteer firefighters in San Francisco to support, the company maintained its distinctive name.

Then came the San Francisco earthquake of 1906. Fireman's Fund almost crumbled along with the city, but with the unwavering support of its agents and policyholders, the company miraculously pulled through and steadily grew throughout the 20th century.

By the time we were contracted by Fireman's Fund in the 1980s, the company had used an employee stock ownership plan to purchase its freedom from parent company American Express and was being led by a young, whip-smart Warren Buffet acolyte named Jay Brown.

We had built an archive for Fireman's Fund and begun to weave together some interesting stories from its history, including unique findings about the company's efforts during the 1906 quake.

Brown, who would have made a great historian, was keenly interested in these stories. Whenever he was in D.C. on business, he would spend a few hours in the archive stacks looking through boxes. We'd set up a table and he'd sit there—this, mind you, is the CEO of the company—poring over documents, intent on understanding how the company had weathered the 1906 earthquake.

By 1989, he had a strong enough command of the materials that he ordered the creation of a comprehensive disaster communications plan.

The wisdom of this decision can't be overstated. Just a few months later, the devastating 1989 Loma Prieta earthquake hit northern California, collapsing the upper deck of the San Francisco-Oakland Bay Bridge and unleashing untold chaos throughout the area.

Brown knew immediately what to do. He remembered the stories about what company leaders did back in 1906.

They had dispatched a telegram to all the company's branches, agents and business associates. It read, "All hands safe and well. Fire now entirely extinguished. Unable to ascertain liabilities until vaults are opened. The Fireman's Fund flag is still flying and nailed to the mast."

The next morning, in accordance with the disaster communications plan, Fireman's Fund beamed via satellite an advertisement that ran in all the major newspapers. It read simply, "Fireman's Fund's flag is still flying and nailed to the mast."

The statement gave Fireman's Fund employees something few other companies could match: a sense of self-esteem and pride. It reinforced the idea that they had risen to meet a similar challenge in 1906 and would do the same in 1989.

And Fireman's Fund did just that, helping San Francisco rise from the rubble by paying out all its claims with speed, grace and dedication.

But the story didn't end there. More than a decade later, in the wake of 9/11, I received a call from Darryl Siry at Fireman's Fund.

He had been reading some of our research about the origins of the company's name in the 19th century and felt it was particularly relevant in the wake of the World Trade Center attacks.

He told me he had been thinking about the heroism of the 9/11 first responders—what they'd done and what they'd endured—and suggested that the company return to its original mission by giving something back to them and their families.

Now that Fireman's Fund was now owned by Allianz, a European financial services corporation, he wanted some help connecting the company's founding ethos with his proposed 9/11 relief work.

We had a perfect link, and Siry took that story—the connection between the company's founding and what was happening at that moment in time—up through the ranks of Allianz's board of directors in Germany, which signed off on the proposal.

The ripple effect of that decision proved to be profound. Not only did the funds help hundreds of first responders, they also helped a new generation of employees and agents reconnect to Fireman's Fund's founding mission.

All the people at Fireman's Fund who handed out checks became symbols of the company's philanthropy. The story humanized the company, a rare feat in any industry. The message was clear and authentic: If we take care of our first responders today, they'll take care of us tomorrow.

International Intrigue: StoryARC for Global Corporations

Our StoryARC methodology would have been invaluable back in 2001, when we helped Fireman's Fund and Allianz understand how a global firm can tell very localized stories. We always accomplished our aims before its advent, but in developing StoryARC we now had a tool that was specifically engineered to tell the stories of global corporations.

If I've learned one thing in conducting oral history interviews across the world, it's this: The farther away you go from an organization's headquarters, the more candid people tend to be.

It's like the old adage: If you want to know what's really going on in your city, head to the next town over and ask somebody.

Same thing with global corporations. If you want to know how popular a particular initiative is or how strong that culture you've been bragging about really is, go out to the most remote place you can find and conduct a StoryARC session. That's where you're going to find the best and most honest responses.

For example, we were contracted by the Whirlpool Corporation in 2010 to create a series of 100th anniversary deliverables that retold its history from an entirely new perspective.

In the past, the history of Whirlpool had been told exclusively with Americans in mind. It was a classic slice of Americana. Real Horatio Alger stuff. All pluck and perseverance. The story of an enterprising family from a small town in Michigan who built a big-time corporation from the ground up.

But now that the company had multiple international subsidiaries and sold its products to consumers around the globe, it needed to realign its story to connect with a more diverse audience. So we packed up our bags and conducted StoryARC sessions around the world, including in India and Italy.

We were interested in hearing international perspectives on key themes that had emerged from our early meetings in the

United States. How—and why—was Whirlpool able to experience such phenomenal global reach? Was there overlap in the way that the company's subsidiaries approached product development and sustainability initiatives? How was its core culture maintained across such long distances? And so on.

We collected a great deal of valuable information and fleshed out our storylines. But we also managed to shed some light on some of the company's enduring unsolved mysteries.

One of my favorites revolved around the company's acquisition of an Italian home-appliance manufacturer. After the deal was struck, U.S. officials planned an elaborate three-day "get to know you" celebration in Italy. The idea was for the United States to bring its leadership team over and have members meet with their Italian counterparts for a weekend of drinking, dining and discussion.

Suffice to say, it didn't go as planned. The Italians seemed disinterested, and the attendance at some events was downright dismal.

This was a mystery to officials in the United States, but when we conducted StoryARC sessions with longtime Italian employees we quickly learned why. The Americans had unwittingly scheduled the meeting right smack dab in the middle of the World Cup.

So whenever the Americans turned to their Italian counterparts to say, "We'll see you downstairs at 5 p.m.," the Italians would turn to each other and groan. Every chance they got, they'd go find the nearest TV. The Americans were left in their seats, all wondering the same thing: "What's wrong with these guys? They don't even have the common courtesy to have a drink or two with us?"

You only get those kinds of stories when you go to the source, which is what we did. And when we came back, we found that we had an extraordinary number of great stories to tell: really clear hinge points, moments of danger, and ultimately some extraordinary moments of triumph.

The company's early foray into China, for example, was a real trial by fire. The team knew that if they didn't succeed, they would have to pack their bags and head back to Michigan with real hell to pay at home.

And then there were some great stories from Mexico, during the company's move into Latin America. Early on, Mexican workers felt so embarrassed by having to wear the company's bright blue safety uniforms that they called them "Pitufos," the Spanish word for Smurf.

And yet it was precisely because Whirlpool was so candid in allowing us to craft a story that revealed all the difficulties of its expansion efforts that the company's eventual global triumphs and solidarity proved so meaningful.

Using our StoryARC methodology, we were able to create a book, online narratives, videos and a set of Web-based employee orientation modules that helped all the company's divisions and acquisitions see themselves as part of a much larger narrative.

Whirlpool isn't unique in this' way. When a corporation goes global, its history is often the last part of its operations to get re-examined. It's the one thing that many companies leave untouched, which is a mistake. Ultimately, it's that new story that most powerfully brings an expanding company together and makes it whole again: one unified organization instead of a fragmented collection of fiefdoms.

A Clock, a Bridge, a Monitor and Thought Clouds in the Sky

I've always said that The History Factory was built by our clients. And as we were busy showing off how our StoryARC could help organizations adapt to changing conditions, the post-2008 period became a hinge point for The History Factory itself.

In late 2008, around the time we were building StoryARC, we were stuck in neutral, in what I like to refer to as our homogenization period.

The culture in our Chantilly office had gotten way too staid. You couldn't go up to the roof anymore and just have a beer. It was hard for many of our new people who lived in downtown D.C. to make the 25-mile trek to Chantilly, so they tended to walk in the door already tired and grumpy. The pace and style of work became tedious and started to feel a bit too archival.

Punch in. Process. Leave at 5 p.m. Day done.

It wasn't for me. And I began to visit our offices in Chantilly less and less. I knew it was time for a change when my wife took a trip out there to pick up an insurance form and came back feeling depressed.

"People didn't look happy," she told me. "It's dark in there and things are getting run down. You need better carpet and a lot more light. You can tell that people just aren't excited to go out there anymore."

Talk about a danger point. The economy was collapsing. We were tightening our belts, and our office felt like a gulag. And here I was locked in an office on Connecticut Avenue in the heart of D.C. with two aspiring movie directors talking about the story architecture of Shakespeare and *The Collected Works of Frank Norris*.

I knew we needed a change. And as I have been wont to do over the years, I decided to blow things up. Clear the decks. Mess up the whole board and see where the pieces would fall.

I started with our logo, an H-shaped bridge with the words "The History Factory" printed underneath.

When we had moved to Chantilly, it served its purpose. It was clean and simple. The H stood for The History Factory and the bridge motif was developed to show how our work spanned the distance between past and future. It was the right logo for a rapidly expanding company in full-on corporate mode.

But now, that H-shaped bridge didn't seem to match up with the exciting things we were creating with StoryARC. It seemed too plain and conventional, so I decided it was time to go in a different direction.

We needed to redesign our website, so we hired a design firm to interview a number of our clients, past and present. When the interviews were completed, the designer told me what I already knew: There was a huge disconnect between how our clients perceived us and the image we were projecting to the world.

Our designer said all of the people he talked to kept coming back to the fact that we were an organization built on creativity, passion and big ideas—and that none of those attributes were reflected in our website and rather austere-looking H-shaped bridge.

We needed something that told a story, that captured not only who we were but where we were going. So we kept the bridge element but scaled it down, transforming it into a platform upon which the rest of the logo would rest. The architectural details we sculpted onto our new bridge included our first logo, back when we were called the Informative Design Group.

But then sitting on top of the bridge was this fantastic collage of symbols. A pair of factory pipes was added to reflect the fact that we created useful products. An old clock tower symbolized time and also had our founding date etched on it. Passing clouds represented our creativity and our constant push to reach new heights.

A thin digital screen reflected our desire to always leverage new technologies. On the screen, hiding below a digital time-line, was our guiding philosophy, Start with the Future and Work Back, spelled out in small letters.

When my wife saw it, she didn't like it. "No, no, no," she said. "No one's going to take you seriously. This isn't you; this is Disney."

At that point, I knew we had it. "That's exactly what I want," I said. "I mean, who's more creative than Disney? Who's more a part of the American landscape? Who runs a better business? Who tells better stories and touches people's lives and creates more everlasting memories than Walt Disney?"

Once the new logo was completed, we had a catalyst to sprint ahead. We kept the archival part of our business in Chantilly, updating the look and feel of the space, but moved all our non-archival staff back to downtown D.C., where we belonged, right in the heart of our nation's capital.

Our new offices are designed to allow all of our people—designers, writers, story architects, archivists, managers—to mingle and share ideas, which is the way it should be. We knocked down the silos and got people collaborating again.

I firmly believe the time and energy that we poured into creating our new logo helped us get there.

When our clients see our logo now, they know what they're going to get from us: a brand-savvy company with creativity to spare that's focused on storytelling and meeting business objectives.

From the moment people see our logo, they say, "That's different. There has to be a great story behind that logo." And the truth of the matter is that there is.

Finding America via Switzerland

Shortly before we began working on StoryARC, EVP and COO Rick Beller and Managing Director Jason Dressel each took some time to develop their own methodologies.

Jason is our business developer, so he created what we call Solutions Mapping™. This is a process in which we sit clients down and physically map out all the communication channels that can carry the content we create.

Solutions Mapping is all about helping clients internally and externally leverage their heritage.

How can a story be used? Where can it be used? Where is it relevant? How can content be repurposed so the message reaches the right people in the right voice and in the right ways?

That's Solutions Mapping.

Meanwhile, Rick, who is a master at consultative selling, developed our Clear Line of Sight™ methodology, which helps clients better understand their messaging and pinpoint its intended audience.

Clear Line of Sight is built to find out exactly what a client wants to accomplish. It sets up a series of targets so that our stories can lock onto them and hit them in the center of the bull's-eye.

It's a methodology that asks our clients important questions, like "What are you trying to say?" "Who are you trying to say it to?" "What do you want to them to do, having heard the message?" And then "What kind of resources do you have to support those goals?"

In combining Clear Line of Sight, StoryARC and Solutions Mapping with our fundamental guiding principle, Start with the Future and Work Back, we have all the tools we need to build deliverables that tell compelling stories and yield targeted results.

Clear Line of Sight informs us about the needs of our audience as well as the messages we need to communicate. Solutions Mapping ensures we're choosing the right deliverables—whether it's an exhibit, a book, a video, Web copy or a combination of these—to properly deliver the message. And then with StoryARC, we have a tool that allows us to collect the right information and build a story that hits the mark.

I knew the importance of all of these methodologies individually, but I didn't realize just how seamlessly they would fit together until 2011, when we were contracted by the Zurich Insurance Group to work on the 100th anniversary of its American business.

I'd go as far as to say we won our Zurich business precisely because we had these three methodologies at our disposal. When we first entered into discussions with Zurich, a faction of the company's internal communication team argued that the company should document its 100-year history with a conventional history book and video.

When we took an early dive into Zurich's history, however, we began to realize that there was much more to Zurich's American story than most people, including some in its Swiss headquarters, ever realized.

On the one hand, we realized the project posed some unique challenges. We were going to need to write a 100-year history of a subsidiary of a Swiss company that most people in the United States had never heard of, let alone felt any connection to. But we soon realized that Zurich had played a major role in insuring some of the most important buildings and projects in the history of the United States.

The Chicago's World Fair. The Hoover Dam. Madison Square Garden. The New York and Chicago subway systems. The Macy's Thanksgiving Day Parade. All were insured or supported in one way or another by Zurich and its legacy companies.

That was a story worth telling. Here was a company whose history was the very fabric of the American experience. Zurich was more American than most American insurance companies.

When we presented this to Zurich's leadership, they were stunned at the storylines we were developing. After we conducted a Clear Line of Sight session, we realized that Zurich's story was going to resonate not only internally as a motivator with its own employees but that it could have a tremendous impact on external audiences and potential clients as well.

Between our Clear Line of Sight and our Solutions Mapping work, we determined that these stories should be communicated through multiple channels. A single internal book simply wouldn't be enough.

Zurich wholeheartedly agreed, and soon we were collaborating with Zurich's communication team to create a multitude of deliverables: an external-facing e-book, a softcover book about the company's anniversary-year celebrations, advertisements that could be placed in newspapers and on the sides of buses, and a series of pop-up exhibits based on quarterly themes.

Every single product served a discrete purpose with a specific audience and a concrete strategic objective in mind.

When we conducted our StoryARC sessions, we unearthed some fascinating findings about the company. Franklin Delano Roosevelt had worked for one of Zurich's legacy companies, Fidelity & Deposit Company of Maryland, before he became the governor of New York in 1928. We tracked down the desk he had used while at Fidelity & Deposit and displayed it in the company's Schaumburg headquarters before donating it, with much media attention, to the FDR Presidential Library and Museum in Hyde Park, New York.

We found some dramatic hinge points as well. Here was a company that helped pioneer automobile insurance in the United States, remained a viable American subsidiary of a European company throughout World War II, and helped modernize some of America's largest urban areas in the 1960s, '70s and '80s.

From our StoryARC sessions and outlines, we were able to team with Publicis, Zurich's agency of record, to generate some truly head-turning ads with pictures of some of America's greatest landmarks as they were being built. One used a shot of the Hoover Dam paired with this phrase: "An insurance policy that held nothing back. Except 9.2 trillion gallons of water."

Another ad included an image of early 20th century workers building a skyscraper. The tagline read, "Why insure people who would scale 100-story structures? Because they're building the country's future."

We took the outlines of these stories and built out four theme-based narratives for Zurich—Our American Experience, Our People, Our Customers, Our Community. We supplemented the stories with images and stories from community events held throughout the anniversary year, showing how people were living out Zurich's values in the present day.

The feedback was tremendous. We hit every target. We clarified Zurich's importance in the U.S. market relative to its top competitors. Client satisfaction and loyalty retention rates rose. Plus, participation in the company's community service initiatives went through the roof, almost doubling Zurich's initial goal targets, and employee engagement scores went up double digits over two years.

Why did our stories resonate so strongly with so many different audiences? Because we took the time to carefully engineer every one of these stories, not only to be great reads but to speak to different audiences in different ways.

In a word, we made them relevant. We uncovered what was an untold history and gave it the Hollywood treatment.

What we learned from Zurich is this: If you get the stories right and use the right kind of architecture, you can use them to build any deliverable you want.

It doesn't matter if it's a film, a book, an exhibit, a conference or Web copy, the outcome is still the same. Our methodologies now allow us to do some amazing things. They allow us to take a client's story, ostensibly load it into a cannon and turn all those knobs just right, so that when we light the wick it's going to land right in the bunker.

What we're looking for—and what StoryARC gives us with startling accuracy and regularity—are stories with impact. Stories that can make an explosion.

StoryARC FOR PRESENTATIONS: THE HOGAN LOVELLS MERGER

Over the years, our emphasis on storytelling has proved particularly useful in transforming rudimentary leadership conferences and engagements into true must-see events. But it wasn't until 2010, when one of our longtime clients, Hogan & Hartson, announced it was merging with the London-based Lovells law firm that we employed StoryARC to program a multi-day company retreat.

The macro theme of the retreat was focused on the concept of "winning"—in getting the partners of both of these prestigious law firms to believe and then act like they were part of one winning team.

For the event flow, we employed a classic three-act structure. Act One was created to build awareness about the histories of the two firms and to inspire people to make a commitment to their new partners. So we opened the conference with a video about international Grand Prix race teams. These were law firms working in a variety of practice areas, so we used this high-charged video to show how all the different elements of a race-car team— the engineers, the designers, the pit crew and the driver—were needed to win a race.

We anchored Act Two with a documentary about Hogan Lovells' client, Ford Motor Company, whose remarkable turnaround orchestrated by Alan Mulally and his leadership team underscored the power of belief, the idea that you have to internalize a goal and make it personal in order to increase your chances of achieving it.

And finally Act Three outlined the vision of what the law firm was going to look like, the goals that it hoped to achieve, and how this shared vision for the future was rooted in the histories of these two great law firms.

It worked beautifully. Lawyers who had never met before walked out of the conference feeling like they'd known each other for years. You could feel the energy, pride and motivation. That's because the event wasn't filled with your typical PowerPoint presentations and handouts. It was built around storytelling and the principle that great stories impel people to act—to go out and make a difference, not only for themselves but for the people they work with as well.

7

AUTHENTICITY SELLS

The Power of Corporate History in an Age of Convergence

I'm intrigued about the prospect of living and working in our increasingly blurred world. Cultures, technologies and economies are all changing so much and at such a rapid clip that traditional borders are all but disappearing.

The global economy is shrinking the distances between "here" and "there." Shared content is erasing the lines between what's "mine" and "yours." And new technologies are eliminating the once-strict divides between words, images and video.

In regard to corporate history, the line once separating the past from the present has all but disappeared as well.

Just look at how we measure time these days. History is no longer simply what happened five years ago or five months ago. It's what happened earlier today—five hours or five minutes ago.

Time is being compressed. History is both then and now. It unfurls on a moment-to-moment basis, constantly being recorded and updated like stock prices gliding along on a news crawl.

In fact, I would argue that if an organization doesn't have more ticks on its timeline—more growth, more change, more achievements—in the last five years than it had in the first 100 years, it's in serious trouble.

And with these changes occurring so rapidly, it's increasingly important that organizations find ways to both capture and disseminate their history in real time.

The future of The History Factory lies in our ability to provide clients with on-demand historical content. I'm talking about data banks of strategically curated materials— what we call content engines—that will allow communicators to instantly preserve and access content to help them meet a particular objective.

Looking to improve employee morale or integrate a new acquisition into your story? We can do both. We will build you a content engine filled with stories, images, videos, timelines and tweets specifically tailored to help you reach each particular goal.

In today's business environment, it's all about speed and usability. Organizations simply don't have the luxury of time anymore, of being able to slowly unveil a new product or insert themselves into the pressing topic of the moment.

Companies need to have reservoirs of curated content at their disposal to ensure they remain an important voice in the conversation.

Silence simply isn't an option anymore. If you're not constantly communicating your story and values, you're on the road to becoming irrelevant.

But I would also argue that organizations need to capture and disseminate the right kind of content in order for it to be of any value.

Like it or not, our communications channels have gone completely democratic. Once a piece of content—whether it's sales figures, a story or an advertising push—finds its way into the ether, there's simply no controlling where it goes and how it will be interpreted. It can go anywhere, including places you never expected it to go. And as it travels along, it'll be accepted or rejected by just about everyone along the way.

For leaders steeped in the command-and-control ways of old, this can be a daunting proposition. But for organizations willing to take the time and expense to curate and disseminate authentic content on a continual basis, this can be an extraordinary opportunity.

As one of my mentors, the legendary adman Arthur Einstein, has drummed into me: People are in search of the real. Given a chance to choose between something authentic and something manufactured, they'll choose the honest thing every time.

What's more authentic, from an organizational perspective, than your own history? A story from 50 years ago is valuable, but one from five days ago can be precious as well. It's real. It happened. It's verifiable. And most important of all, it's uniquely yours.

Tell timely stories about your organization in the right ways and you can craft content that truly resonates. It can permeate in ways that were simply impossible for the old command-and-control system to ever match.

An Unexpected Flight Path: Lockheed Martin Finds Its Voice

Our work with Lockheed Martin represents a perfect example of how we not only can document history in real time but also deploy content in extraordinarily timely and strategic ways.

We were approached by Lockheed Martin in 2011, one year before its 100th anniversary, to build a story bank of 100 narratives highlighting the company's many contributions to aeronautics, civil defense and space exploration.

We had so much content from the distant past that we could have easily ignored what Lockheed was working on at the moment and still created a jaw-dropping corporate heritage project. But we didn't. We focused on the present as much as we did the past.

We wrote an array of stories about Lockheed innovations, some of which were still in development. We profiled the company's newest fighter, the F-35B, its cutting-edge energy-efficient Ocean Thermal Energy Conversion (OTEC), and its Infantry Immersion trainers, which re-create the rigors of war in virtual battlefields.

Those stories were carefully unveiled on a public-facing website throughout the anniversary year, many of them tapping into the water-cooler discussions of the hour.

As more pictures of Mars pinged their way back to Earth, readers could peruse stories documenting Lockheed's early contributions to the exploration of the Red Planet. Interested in the 50th anniversary of the Cuban Missile Crisis? We had stories ready to go about surveillance planes and the U-2 "Dragon Lady." Talk of cyber security on Page One? Go read about Lockheed's crime-fighting NexGen Cyber Innovation and Technology Center.

Our stories were so relevant that all Lockheed needed to do was post them, and mainstream and social media outlets picked them up. Everyone latched on to the stories and pushed them deeper into the public's consciousness.

We wrote a story, for example, about Kelly Johnson, the engineer who ran Lockheed's top-secret Skunk Works division. It was designed to speak to young engineers, to show them that Lockheed Martin had a long track record of embracing engineers who wanted to break barriers and create new technologies.

After it was released, I spoke to a 29-year-old engineer who had read it and relayed the entire story back to me as if he'd memorized it. I'd hear Lockheed Martin stories at dinner parties and in casual conversations with people you'd never dream would have been interested in the defense industry.

Why? Because we engineered those stories to be relevant—to be interesting and timely enough that people would pass them along, around their dinner tables and on social media.

The stories didn't parrot the discussion of the hour; they added context to them, which helped readers across the globe not only realize Lockheed's tremendous contributions but generate a sense of excitement for what was yet to come.

Working on Deadline: History as Advertising Support

My interest in developing real-time history programs dates back to our early work in the banking industry. The 1980s and early 1990s were an extraordinary growth period for banks. Every time we completed a project for one of our clients, they'd go out and acquire another bank. And then we'd have to quickly integrate the history of their new acquisitions into their larger narratives.

In the days of telephone and fax, this was no easy task. But it taught us the importance of operating with speed and efficiency, in rejecting the often-deliberate pace of academia for something more akin to journalists working on a tight deadline.

One of my favorite stories involves our work with what was then Fleet/Norstar Financial Group in the wake of a mini bank run in the 1990s.

It all started when a small industrial bank in Providence, Rhode Island, overextended itself so much that it was forced to shut its doors. That bank's deposits weren't federally insured, so the bank's poor depositors came running like a scene out of *It's a Wonderful Life.*

When word got out, a mini bank run spread across Providence. Confidence was shattered. Everyone wanted their money, whether it was federally insured or not. And thus our client, Fleet/Norstar, found itself inundated with frantic calls from worried customers.

In all honesty, Fleet was such a well-secured and well-run organization that its clients didn't have anything to worry about, but Fleet wanted to nip the panic in the bud, so it charged its ad agency with creating a campaign to calm people down as quickly as possible.

The ad agency set out to draft an ad assuring customers that Fleet/Norstar had a long and dependable track record of keeping people's money safe. Finding a way to come up with an authentic image that conveyed that idea, however, proved elusive.

Fleet/Norstar's ad agency knew we were managing the company's archives, so a harried creative director called us to see if we could help. They had comped up an ad that read, "If this is your first mortgage, don't worry; it's not ours." And there, right next to the copy, was a crude drawing of what they imagined an ancient mortgage to look like, randomly dated "1847."

One of our archivists booted up his computer, opened Fleet/Norstar's archive database and pulled up a copy of a mortgage from 1847.

Within five minutes, the image of the historical document was faxed to the ad agency, and about 30 seconds later, the phone rang. The creative director on the other end was ecstatic. All you could hear for the first 10 seconds or so was a loud whoop of excitement.

To this day, I still remember his exact words. "I've been in this business for a long time," he said. "This is the most gratifying moment in my career. You made my idea become real. It was like I dreamt it, and you instantly made it happen."

After the ads launched, everyone calmed down. The phones stopped ringing. Trust was regained. We would go on to provide advertising support for everyone from Marriott to Craftsman, but our experience with Fleet/Norstar provided our first evidence that history in real time was not only possible but also a potentially invaluable asset to our clients.

Arabian Tales: Saudi Aramco and the King Abdullah University of Science and Technology

In the years that followed, our ability to quickly access and deliver historical content only improved, thanks to new technologies including our LuminARC archival program and digital story banks.

However, I felt we were in a unique position to do something more: to actually go out and capture history as it was unfolding—in real time.

This was a bold leap for a self-described corporate heritage organization. Historians tend to analyze and interpret, not obtain and record. But I knew our extensive experience creating videos, conducting oral histories, and leveraging digital technologies provided the right mix of tools and skills for us to become documentarians as well.

We knew what stories from history were worth recording and telling, so why not find a way to capture those moments as they were occurring?

Up until the late 1990s, this sort of project would have been impossible. We would have needed the equivalent of a full-fledged news crew to do it right. The advent of high-end digital cameras and thimble-sized microphones, however, changed everything. I watched as lone entrepreneurial-minded journalists became roving one-man movie studios and realized it was time to put my idea into practice.

I have one of our longest-standing and most valuable clients, Saudi Aramco, to thank for the opportunity to show what we could do.

We first earned Saudi Aramco's business in the late 1990s. In the 1930s, the Saudi government had granted exploration rights to American oil companies, which struck oil and negotiated concessions that gave them some ownership rights over the company. As a result, Saudi Aramco's history had been written from an American perspective, not from the Saudi point of view. So company leaders went shopping. They traveled around the world interviewing different agencies to see who would be best suited to write a book about its history.

When they came to us, we asked them why they wanted to write a book in the first place. What, in other words, was this book being written to achieve?

They asked us what we would need to find an answer. We said that we'd have to visit Saudi Arabia to conduct research and talk to people on the ground. It was a classic Start with the Future and Work Back proposal. They were sold.

Over a 12-month period, our team of researchers and writers shuttled back and forth to the Middle East, immersing themselves in Saudi culture and learning why Saudi Aramco needed a book. It became clear that this was a story that could help a wide range of Saudi and other global audiences understand the role that Saudi Aramco played in the kingdom's development.

We ended up writing three books in both English and Arabic: a two-volume definitive history of Saudi Aramco for internal and global audiences, and two books for Saudi Arabia's youth.

With the book projects, we gained our client's trust, which in the Arab world is a precious commodity. So when Saudi Aramco's 75th anniversary approached, company officials reached out to us again, hoping we could come up with a comprehensive anniversary plan, to be anchored by a special event for King Abdullah to commemorate the anniversary.

From our previous work, we knew the company history inside out, so we had an answer for them almost immediately. In 1947, the King's father and founder of Saudi Arabia, King Abdulaziz Al-Saud, had visited Saudi Aramco. It was a big deal. We found this striking photograph of King Abdulaziz sitting there with all of these young children of Aramco's American employees surrounding him.

We worked with Saudi Aramco to come up with an event that would recreate that experience in Dhahran and bring back the children in the photograph, people now in their 70s and 80s. The ceremony would be called Walking in the Footsteps, which would basically allow King Abdullah to retrace the steps his father had made 60 years ago.

Well, he came. And the first half of the ceremony was a very lively extravaganza of grand performances and multimedia shows. King Abdullah, who was in his 80s at the time, sat patiently and watched. But when the children from 1947 arrived, he became more animated. He talked to them all and proceeded to do a sword dance called Al Ardha. He waved the sword and danced like a man half his age. It was incredible to see, and we recorded it all for posterity.

During this same time frame, it has been said that King Abdullah had a vision telling him to rebuild the great house of wisdom that had been the seat of math and science for the entire Middle East in Saudi Arabia. So he went to his closest advisors and asked them to build the King Abdullah University of Science and Technology (KAUST.)

It was a monumental task. King Abdullah wanted it built in three years and charged Saudi Aramco with making it happen. We were engaged to document the three-year process in real time.

A massive team of educators, architects and building contractors was working 24/7 on site in Thuwal, north of Jeddah on the coast of the Red Sea, and at locations around the world.

Whenever there was a major meeting or development, our team was there, with camera or notepad in hand.

We documented the entire process with video, audio, oral histories and stories—as well as the actual grand opening of the university in 2009. We wrote a book about the project but also handed over a vast reservoir of firsthand research to KAUST Library to serve as the university's foundational archive.

The Great Recession: A Hinge Point for Corporate Heritage

Our work documenting the creation of the King Abdullah University of Science and Technology was completed shortly after the start of the Great Recession, which has proven to be a rather important pivot point in how organizations view their history.

I don't think one can overestimate to what degree the 2008 mortgage crisis and ensuing recession affected corporate America. To me, it was a little bit like an earthquake. Companies had been building so fast and so high and in so many different directions that they didn't realize just how far they'd come.

Then 2008 hit. It was a shock. Some organizations fractured. Some came crashing down. But those that survived intact tended to come out of it feeling a great deal of anxiety. We saw an extraordinary uptick in calls from new and former clients, all of whom seemed to be saying the same thing: "We have to rebuild," they told us. "We have to reconnect. We have to find some kind of solid ground to stand on before we push ahead again."

I've seen this phenomenon before. Short bouts of uncertainty like this occurred in the early 1990s, after the dot-com bubble burst, and post-9/11. None of those situations, however, mirrored what happened after 2008.

Employees felt they didn't have the kind of job security they thought they did. Client loyalty became more fragile. And companies looked for something, anything, that wouldn't shift below their feet.

So they turned, as companies are prone to do in periods of uncertainty, to their history for guidance and assurance.

It was instinctual, like when you slam on your car brakes and you stretch your hand out to brace whoever is sitting in the passenger seat. History gave our clients that sense of protection.

And when companies slowed down for a moment, they realized that their history—all they'd accomplished in recent years—was right on top of them and they didn't know what to do with it.

The history was just too close. It was a jumble. It was a blur. No one had a point of view on what was worth preserving and communicating and what wasn't.

Which is when we showed up with our Start with the Future and Work Back philosophy and our suite of StoryARC, Clear Line of Sight and Solutions Mapping methodologies.

Following the Great Recession, we were called for more consultations than at any point in our history. Our job? Provide a little clarity to the blur.

We did what we always did. We helped companies see the relevance of their history. We showed them how to convert their historical content into engaging stories. We built archives, conducted oral history programs, wrote books, shot videos, developed digital content and created exhibits.

Then, we mapped out all the places and channels where they needed to send those stories: social media, internal microsites, recruiting materials, training modules—anywhere and everywhere they needed to go.

Our real-time history work still ran on parallel tracks. There were projects that demanded delivery of content in real time and those that required we document content in real time.

Then came a call in 2010 from Adobe, which gave us an opportunity to do something we'd never done before: merge the documentation and dissemination of real-time history into a single project.

Behind the Splash Screen: Humanizing Adobe

Adobe's aim, as it approached the 20th anniversary of Photoshop in 2010, was to tell Photoshop's history in a way that appealed to both longtime and brand-new users, while calling attention to the release of its newest product, Creative Suite 5 (CS5).

That was a challenge in itself, but to complicate matters, an anti-Photoshop movement was brewing at Apple. Steve Jobs made it a point to publicly criticize the performance and security of Adobe products, particularly Flash.

Jobs' attacks had the potential to deliver a serious blow to Adobe's reputation with Apple supporters. But the interesting thing was that almost everyone within Adobe was an Apple loyalist who supported many of Jobs' philosophies.

Adobe believed that if it celebrated the 20th anniversary of Photoshop using the stories of its designers and programmers, then techies, as well as the general public, would connect with the passion and innovation within Adobe's ranks.

And what a dramatic story the Photoshop team told. Just as Adobe was halfway through programming its new CS5 product for Apple's Carbon operating system, Apple unexpectedly introduced a new OS called Cocoa. With a product launch looming, Adobe had the herculean task of having to start from scratch to make CS5 compatible with Cocoa.

Of course, we collected plenty of war stories. More importantly, we asked everyone the simple question: "Why do you do this? What's your motivation for doing this?"

The responses we received were mesmerizing. People teared up during these interviews. Nobody was coached; they just shared their individual stories.

They talked about tinkering around with computers as children with their parents. They talked about the pain of being outsiders and outcasts in school. They talked about art, technology and computers with such passion that it was impossible not to like them and not to feel more connected with Adobe as a company.

The resulting Photoshop 20th anniversary social media campaign was called "The People Behind the Splash Screen" and was based on the challenges and triumph of completing CS5 by its designated launch date.

Our first "Behind the Splash Screen" video vignette received more than 1,000 "likes" within minutes of posting, and over 20,000 YouTube views in its first week online. The number of views continued to grow, persuading Apple devotees to give a second look to Adobe but, more importantly, preserving a key moment in Adobe's history.

History on Demand: The Birth of the Content Engine

If our work with Adobe taught us anything, it's that the age of shallow content is over. If you want to generate truly valuable content, you have to give people the opportunity to go as deep into a client's story as possible.

Just look at how ancestry.com has evolved in recent years. In the early days, all ancestry.com did was help people to identify the names of their ancestors and where they came from. Today, that's shallow content, simply a starting point leading to deeper finds.

If you know your ancestors' names and where they came from, then ancestry.com will point you toward the name and images of the boat that carried them here, the port they entered, and the neighborhood where they settled.

Put these pieces together, and what do you have? A historical narrative.

Why do people get so obsessed with epics like *Star Wars* and *The Lord of the Rings*? Because they allow people to go as deep into those worlds as they want. You want a map of Middle Earth? You can get it. Interested in the schematics for an X-wing fighter? You can get it. The content for both worlds not only runs deep but is also easily accessible.

I've long believed that corporations need to begin thinking along similar lines, looking for ways to allow people to connect on a personal level with their organizations in much the same way that individuals can plumb the depths of their friends and families' lives on Facebook.

But in order to provide those opportunities, companies need content. Lots of content, from the past and closer to the present, which must then be curated so that it's easy for a company's communication team to access and use.

In 2013, my theories were confirmed when we brought in a group of University of Chicago professors who focus on entrepreneurs and technology, to participate in an internal colloquium built exclusively for The History Factory. After hearing our story and conducting a daylong discussion, our collaborators made it clear that our growth and the growth of our clients was predicated on how quickly and comprehensively we could get content into the hands of our customers and show them how to properly use it in this digital age.

In order to make that happen, we decided to build what we call a content engine, which is an application—a filter—that distills the vast amount of information found in a digital archive into an aggregation of data curated to meet a particular growth objective.

Interested in extending your brand? Good. We can help. We can have one of our curators mine your archive and extract the most relevant stories, images, videos, timelines, figures, schematics and tweets from your organization's history.

Your brand-focused content engine will house content from the distant past all the way up to the present day, but it will be displayed on your desktop via a user-friendly interface that's as easy to navigate as any search engine.

With a content engine, you don't have to understand archival subgroups, record types or formats. Just simple tabs clustered around that central theme of branding: brand logos, advertising campaigns, marketing language, press releases, external campaigns.

Click on one and you see large thumbnail previews of a given document or images laid out like icons on your phone.

A content engine is virtuous in the sense that the more you use it, the smarter it gets. Not unlike Amazon, it says, "You looked for these things. Maybe you're interested in these other things." Once you use it, your search information is preserved in the database.

We decided to build it atop our LuminARC system, so that it would be easier to take materials out of a client's archive as well as accurately file new content back into the archives. Thus, it's a perfect two-way system for collecting and communicating content.

For me, content engines represent the first step toward my long-held desire to create self-curating historical databases. Today, our clients still rely on our curatorial team to sift through their archives and populate the content engines.

But in the future, as we develop new algorithms and blend those with the rich amount of information we can glean from big data, we will be able to build content engines that operate by themselves.

They will absorb all the daily activities of a given organization—the reports, the stories, the press releases, the images—distill them down to what's potentially valuable, and then dispense that content at the right time and on the right date.

Think about it. Today, we all receive birthday congratulations and coupons from retailers. But what if savvy companies found ways to curate personalized content about their history and link it up with the interests of their followers? Say you're a New York Yankees fan. The day the Yankees clinch the division, you receive personalized historical content from an insurance company detailing how it insured the old Yankee Stadium for a 15-year period in the 1960s and 1970s. You'd remember that, wouldn't you?

It's just going to evolve from there. It's going to lead to a point where people who work inside a company will be able to create direct links with people outside the company. If you're a Tesla buff and you're constantly pinning Tesla images to your Pinterest board, wouldn't it be cool to have a direct link to Tesla's design department? To receive something from its history—some image or quote—that magnifies and strengthens that relationship?

And thus you can begin to see how the history of organizations can be absorbed by their customers in authentic yet organic ways. Because if recent years have taught us anything, it's that if the content is unique enough and authentic enough, people will gravitate toward it.

The companies that capture their history—not just in the distant past but what happened 30 minutes ago—will have the largest bank of content to draw from. And it's those companies, the ones with the deepest content, that will ultimately be able to make the deepest connections.

The Age of Convergence: Riffing on the Past and Future

I know all of this rapid change is unsettling for some, but the truth of the matter is that we've been working toward this moment since The History Factory was established in 1979.

As I've said before, when we use our Start with the Future and Work Back methodology, what we're really doing is uncovering continuities between the past, present and future. The rigid concepts of "then" and "now" soften to such a degree that future goals simply become an extension of past achievements.

We forge connections. We connect the dots. We make the past relevant again. And soon our clients find they have compelling, highly targeted stories to tell, which can help drive them toward new goals and greater growth.

There's nothing that we do at The History Factory that isn't predicated on the notion that you can combine two seemingly disparate things and make them far more useful than the individual parts.

Old and new. Word and image. Physical and digital. Past and future.

Just look at our deliverables. Our archives are organized like academic libraries but offer the feel and ease of use of a world-class search engine. Our stories blend historical facts with all the hallmarks of a great piece of literature. Our exhibits blend videos, text and imagery to tell stories in three dimensions.

The History Factory is, if nothing else, an integrated company built for an integrated world.

Today, if an organization wants to remain relevant, it has to constantly align and realign its story, culture and philosophies to the rapid changes occurring all around it.

It has to be equipped to function in the blur.

For me, it all comes back to music. I think history has a certain musicality to it. It's one long guitar riff, one sound influenced by some other chord that came before it.

When Eric Clapton plays the lead guitar solo of "Sunshine of Your Love," he's cleverly riffing on "Blue Moon." Same thing when an organization pushes toward a new objective. It's building on something—some element of its history—and riffing on it in a way that makes it both new and old at the same time.

Which is why I've always wanted The History Factory to feel like playing in a band. You have different instruments, you have different styles, but when we come together, we can play some beautiful music.

That's why I do what I do. Sometimes to take a giant leap forward, you have to take a quick glance back. You have to remember who and what came before.

It's humbling to think that if The History Factory didn't exist, the histories of some of the world's greatest organizations would have disappeared. Think about all those achievements and insights vanishing into the darkness. And all those great stories of innovation and sheer perseverance in the face of tragedy slipping away.

I just don't want those stories to go away.

I don't want the melodies and lyrics of corporate America to get lost. I want to preserve them for future generations, so they'll not only know them but be inspired by them. I want the old music, in the right hands, to generate new sounds.

I want the music to keep playing, both in your house and in ours.

ACKNOWLEDGMENTS

I've always felt that The History Factory must be a great idea because, despite my ineptitude as a businessman and lots of silly mistakes, I've been unable to kill it. In truth, over the years I've been assisted on all counts by a colorful cast of characters.

Credit must be given to my cofounder, Tom West, who stood shoulder-to-shoulder with me for the company's first formative decade. An artist by skill and temperament, Tom selflessly shouldered the mundane but essential day-to-day administrative duties that I've always been loath to address.

A lot of extremely talented people have made contributions to The History Factory, but nobody has surpassed Alden Hathaway for his commitment, loyalty and longevity. Alden's Yankee skepticism and Protestant work ethic have made him a role model for generations of staff members. He's been the contrarian when necessary, and for that—among many other wonderful qualities—he's an invaluable comrade and good friend.

The History Factory attracted amazing professionals who understood us and helped us succeed. Lynn Shepard was our first exhibit fabricator. Jim Monteleone was our first marketing consultant. Leo Mullen designed a sophisticated identity for our fledgling company that gave us gravitas with large corporate clients. Mike Neff was a patient longtime print vendor. Even after 25-plus years, I look forward to seeing John South and Donny Lanham at the holiday party, if only because we're the oldest guys there. And finally, there's the new kid on the block, Han Seok, our trusted technology partner.

There's an old adage that says you don't do business with friends but you make friends through business. I'm grateful to those individuals who took The History Factory with them as they progressed through their illustrious careers. Ron Culp, Wendi Strong, Bob Libbey, Anne McCarthy, Liz Ingoldsby, Rob Doughty and Ed Burke always called as soon as they landed their next big assignments.

Hannah Warmanen got my book project off the ground. Margaux Bergen picked up the ball and brought the book to completion with the able editing of Michelle Witt and design of Linda McNamara. I was encouraged along the way by Michael Leland, Jason Dressel and Tim Schantz. And if it hadn't been for Rick Beller, there's a very good likelihood that this history of The History Factory might have been a postmortem.

Peter Gianopulos goaded, provoked, inspired, energized, consoled and ultimately scribed my incoherent and—at times—hostile ramblings. Peter selflessly risked his considerable reputation as a writer, set aside his justifiable pride, and dragged me kicking and screaming through the process because he truly believed that capturing my story was a worthwhile endeavor. You are a brave soldier, Peter G, for which you have earned both my admiration and appreciation.

I'm forever indebted to Doug Caulkins, who nurtured academically rigorous creativity, and Arthur Einstein, who inspired a steadfast belief in the power of authenticity.

Finally, I'm thankful for my parents, who for many years had no idea what I did for a living . . . but were proud of me anyway.

Washington, D.C.
December 2015

INDEX